BELIEFS OF A UNITED METHODIST CHRISTIAN

Third Edition

Emerson S. Colaw

DISCIPLESHIP RESOURCES

MATERIALS FOR GROWTH IN CHRISTIAN FAITH AND LIFE

P.O. Box 189 • 1908 Grand Avenue
Nashville, TN 37202 • Phone (615) 340-7285

Also, read the companion book, *The United Methodist Primer*, by Chester E. Custer. (#DR024B, available from Discipleship Resources)

Unless otherwise indicated, all scriptural quotations are taken from the Revised Standard Version of the Holy Bible.

Library of Congress Catalog Card Number: 86-51661

ISBN 0-88177-025-6

DR025B

CONTENTS

THE IMPORTANCE OF "DOING THEOLOGY"

I have a conviction that Protestant laity can do creative thinking about theology. This may seem to them, at first, a boring, frustrating enterprise. One minister is quoted as saying, "I love flowers, but I hate botany; I love religion, but I hate theology." It is true that theology can often be dull and has sometimes been unChristian as we have warred with each other over our differing beliefs. But the answer to poor theology must be good theology, not *no* theology. In any case, all people think theological thoughts. *Theology* comes from two Greek words: *Theos,* meaning God, and *logos,* meaning word or rational thought. Theology, therefore, is a word or rational thought about God.

I know many who are inclined to say, "Well, it doesn't matter what we teach just as long as we do the right thing." This is a dangerous half-truth. It does not represent tolerance but indifference. What we do is ultimately determined by what we think and what we hold to be of supreme value. When we are faced with the problem of deciding how to act in a given situation, we must have some idea of what ends we wish to obtain, what values we hope to gain from the solution. Furthermore, we must have some outline as to the best means of achieving these values. All of this is theology, whether it be implicit or explicit. The varying political systems in the world are increasingly aware that there is no simple distinction between what a person believes and what that person does! All governments and institutions rely upon propaganda. Propaganda is a concerted effort to change what people think. Political leaders know that if they can change our thoughts, they can change our actions.

Christian theology is nothing more nor less than the attempt to change our thinking so we will act as Christians. It is the believers who have convictions to live by and die for. The central question has become, "What do you believe?" No question goes deeper.

We all know, of course, that real faith is more than a matter of reason, more than a question of correct intellectual belief. Genuine faith originates in the unique action of God's grace, in the experience of redemptive love that precedes and permits belief. Faith is much more than believing *in* the Christian life: it *is* that life lived in creative surrender of mind, body, emotions, and will to the divine grace. Christian faith has no reality apart from a response to the descent of God's love! Yet careful thought and right thinking precede this moment of acceptance of God's gift. John Wesley, founder of the Methodist movement, had a conviction that "Christ had saved him," but he also had traveled a long road of study and prayer, preparing for the moment of encounter with the living Christ. As a consequence, he was deeply concerned with sound theology.

The earliest agenda of Wesley's Conferences focused on three basic questions:*

1. What to teach? (the substance of the gospel)
2. How to teach? (the proclamation of the gospel)
3. What to do? (the gospel in action)

He was concerned that his preachers be sound in doctrine. He provided guidance for them in the publication of *Forty-four Sermons* and *Explanatory Notes Upon the New Testament*. The *Sermons* and the *Notes* formed the standard for doctrinal correctness in the early Methodist Church. In 1946 the United Brethren and the Evangelical Churches merged. Over the next few years the Board of Bishops prepared a new Confession with sixteen Articles which was presented to the EUB General Conference of 1962. In 1968 the Evangelical United Brethren Church and the Methodist Church merged to form The United Methodist Church. Again a new theological statement was formulated by a Theological Study Commission on Doctrine and Doctrinal Standards. The 1984 General Conference established an-

---

*For an inspiring collection of John and Charles Wesley's own nuggets and answers, see *Wesley Speaks on Christian Vocation* by Paul Wesley Chilcote (Discipleship Resources, #DR041B).

other Commission to reflect on our theological tradition and offer to the 1988 General Conference a revised statement of our beliefs. This illustrates how thinking theologically within The United Methodist Church is an ongoing process.

This book, based upon a theological statement approved by the General Conference, is an invitation to pastors, congregations, and individuals to become involved in the task of "doing theology" within the United Methodist tradition. To take this task seriously could lead to a quickening of the Spirit within our denomination.

Every pastor has encountered the question: "What do we believe as United Methodists?" This volume, drawing upon ideas and concepts developed by the Theological Commission established by General Conference, is designed to be read, pondered, and discussed. The reader is encouraged to experience the excitement of learning and thinking about our theological heritage and defining what that means today.

Please observe that the title of this volume is not: *United Methodist Beliefs*. Rather, it is: *Beliefs of a United Methodist Christian*. Methodism stands in the mainstream of Christian tradition, yet each member must conclude what is essential in his/her faith pilgrimage. There is no "litmus test" of orthodoxy which every United Methodist must pass. As you will note in reading the book, we hold all of the central truths of the faith to be relevant. The sovereignty of God, the uniqueness of Jesus Christ, the presence of the Holy Spirit are beliefs which we feel are of supreme importance. At the same time, we acknowledge a rich diversity in the way we speak of these central doctrines. Hence, the book is quite simply, "Beliefs of *a* United Methodist Christian."

There is no escaping the necessity to speak of convictions and beliefs, emphases and directions, which we hold in common. At the same time, we must recognize that without our denomination there is doctrinal diversity. There is a willingness to think and let think.

There is a well-known phrase that describes us: "In essentials unity, in non-essentials diversity, in all things charity." The unity we seek requires neither an uncritical acceptance of any point of view, nor a rigid formulation of doctrine. We ask for testimonies of faith rather than tests of faith. To those who belong to the Confessional denominations, where everyone must give assent to the same Confession of Faith, our approach must seem inefficient and chaotic. The value of our doctrinal style is that our theologizing takes place within a situation of doctrinal diversity which produces fruitful tension. This can lead us to understand our faith in such a way that it will stimulate each of us to vital worship and celebration, significant evangelistic outreach, and meaningful social and missional application.

Someone has pointed out that General Motors will never make the mistake of offering only one model for its constituency with the implied attitude, "Buy it or walk." And we can't take that attitude, "If you don't like the way we say things, go somewhere else." There is, of course, a danger in diversity. It is that we may splinter and fragment the unity of the Body of Christ. But we take the risk in order that we may reap the rewards of a vital church, alive with ferment and dialogue, sometimes moving off in all directions, but illustrating so richly the truth of Paul's assertion that there are different gifts, different ways of serving God, but it is the same God whose purpose is achieved through them all.

The president of Hebrew Union College, in an address which I heard, said that some Jews wish to deny their Jewishness or say, "I'm Reformed," or "I'm Orthodox." "But when Moses led the Israelites from Egyptian bondage," he reminded his audience, "every Jew was there. When Joshua possessed the promised land, every Jew was there. When they were led into dispersion, and then came back to rebuild the city, every Jew was there. When the concentration camps with their gas ovens were built, every Jew was there. When the dream and longing of the centuries was fulfilled, and Israel was established again—reclaiming a barren country, planting the vineyards and groves—every Jew was there!"

We can remind ourselves—when John Wesley wrote to George Shadford saying, "I turn you loose on the great continent of America. Publish your message in the open face of the sun and do all the good you can"—that every United Methodist was there. When Otterbein, and three others, joined in laying their hands on Francis Asbury's head, thus consecrating him as a bishop, every United Methodist was there. When E. Stanley Jones writes *The Way,* a book of faith and vision, every United Methodist is in it. We have a rich diversity and pluralism in heritage, doctrine, and present practice that constitutes not a threat but a promise. Our controversy, our debates, our varied styles and emphases, our probing and seeking, reflect a healthy body.

We are not necessarily one in doctrine, but we are one in hope—that the kingdoms of this world shall become the kingdom of our Christ. And through it all there is, as Paul phrased it, "the operation of the same Spirit."

CHAPTER ONE

HOW BELIEFS
ARE FORMED

 nited Methodists have their own way of
"doing theology." In the 1984 *Discipline*
(p. 78ff) there is a section titled *Doctrinal
Guidelines in The United Methodist Church.*
The text asks how doctrinal reflection
and construction can be fruitful and fulfilling. The text answers in
terms of our free inquiry within the boundaries defined by four main
sources and guidelines: scripture, tradition, experience, and reason.

First, there is *scripture*. The statement from the *Discipline* reminds
us that as we immerse ourselves in the biblical testimony, as we open
our minds and hearts to the Word of God through the words of
persons inspired by the Holy Spirit, faith is born and nourished.
Discipleship begins with a study of the Word of God. Wherever you
see an alive, vital church you will see a church that has groups who
study the Bible with a significant degree of seriousness and a pastor
who not only understands the importance of biblical preaching, but
practices it!

Second, there is *tradition*. Our Roman Catholic friends have a
greater sense of tradition than do most Protestants. But all of us have a
feeling that indeed we are surrounded by a "great cloud of witnesses." When asking questions about the faith, become conversant
with what was taught by the leaders of previous generations. The
Discipline tells us that "traditions are the residue of corporate experience of earlier Christian communities. A critical appreciation of them
can enlarge our vision and enrich faith in God's provident love"
(p. 79). Some cultures have great respect for the wisdom of the elders.

1

We passed through an era in our own national life when we used the phrase "Never trust anyone over thirty." Fortunately, that time has passed, and we now realize our dependence upon the insights and knowledge gained by previous generations which are made available to us. Whenever you encounter some new idea, ask if this is consistent with the best of what the leaders of the church have taught through the centuries.

Third is *experience*. As you think about the faith, start with your own experience. There is a tendency on the part of persons who have had a life-changing experience of God to assume that every other person must experience it the same way. There is an old story of an intoxicated person who fell into a well. As he swam around, trying to save himself, he began to pray and suddenly had a marvelous conversion experience. He was then rescued but thereafter insisted others should fall into the well so they could have the same experience that had come to him. There are varieties of religious experience. I grew up in a devout home, attended institutes and youth camps in the summer and revivals in the winter. I have the positive memory of kneeling at an altar of prayer, seeking an experience with God. In my senior year in high school I made a decision to study for the Christian ministry. As I look back over my faith pilgrimage, however, I cannot point to any one moment when I became a Christian. There have been times when I have been very conscious of the presence of God, the guidance of the Holy Spirit, the power of prayer. There have also been occasions of spiritual drought. Through it all I have been sustained by a continuing commitment to find and do the will of God.

I have an older brother who is also an ordained minister. His experience differs from mine. When he finished school, he went into business, stopped attending church, and was quite indifferent to the things of religion for a period of some years. Then he came back to the church, experienced a dramatic conversion, and felt the call to Christian ministry. He can identify the time and place where he was converted. I sometimes envy him. But nothing can change my own walk with God. It is *my* experience. Test all doctrines by your own experience. There is validity in this process. Incidentally, studies show that only about one out of six faithful, practicing Christians can point to a dramatic moment of conversion. As suggested in Chapter 8 on Conversion, both the "sudden, dramatic" kind and the "gradual, cumulative" experience are equally important.

Fourth is *reason.* "Christian doctrines which are developed from Scripture, tradition, and 'experience' must be submitted to critical analysis so that they may commend themselves to thoughtful persons as valid. This means that they must avoid self-contradiction and take due account of scientific and empirical knowledge, and yet we recognize that revelation and 'experience' may transcend the scope of reason" (p. 81, *1984 Discipline*).

Christian faith does not require that we do violence to our own sense of what is reasonable. God has given to each of us a mind, and we are exhorted to love the Lord our God with heart, soul, and *mind.*

Many factors influenced Wesley's religious development. He was a product of the Church of England. He was a graduate of Oxford University. He was persuaded by Reformation theology, particularly Luther's insistence upon the biblical norm that the "just shall live by faith." He was indebted to the "New Life in the Spirit" movements, such as the Moravians who reassured him as to the importance of the inner experience. His heart had been "strangely warmed" at Aldersgate. But Wesley was also influenced by the Renaissance writers such as Erasmus who talked of the glory of the lighted mind. Out of this came his awareness of free will. God does not coerce us. We are not automatons. The Holy Spirit may be persuading the heart to faith, but finally we must make a decision as to whether we will accept or reject God's gracious offer of salvation.

These four standards are of critical importance in the process of becoming disciples. They become our resources for "doing theology." Using them as tools on the pilgrimage of faith will bring rich results. Doctrines and beliefs are not something just to be learned from a book. It is not sufficient even to memorize some of the historic creeds, important as they may be in helping the church remember who it is and what it believes. Belief is something all persons must hammer out for themselves as they go to the wellspring of our faith, the Bible. Belief is deepened as we gain familiarity with what Christian people in every age have set forth in creeds, confessions of faith, doctrines, and liturgies. This is using tradition. Belief is confirmed as we examine our own life in Christ which is our personal experience. "Such experience opens faith's eyes to living truth in Scripture, informs and guides the Christian conscience in ethical decisions, and illumines the Christian understanding of God and creation" (*1984 Discipline*, p. 80). And finally, belief is expressed as we use our minds, our sense of the reasonable, to provide clarity and credibility to what we believe and what we teach.

Thus far, in examining how beliefs are formed, the emphasis has been upon the individual search for faith. But only as Christians come into fellowship together can they find the strength to serve Christ in the world. Discipleship becomes a reality as a person becomes related to a group where spiritual interest is stimulated. One of the more promising developments in the contemporary church has been the emergence of the small-group movement. Using various names such as "Covenant Discipleship," "The Twelve," "Yokefellow," "Walk to Emmaus," "Bethel Bible" (or some similar disciplined Bible study approach), these groups offer a structured pattern of prayer, study, and fellowship. The fellowship, however, is more than the casual conversation about weather and sports. Using the New Testament pattern of *koinonia,* there is mutual concern, sharing of personal need, openness to criticism and suggestion, and the development of an accountable attitude where each person can be an authentic self.

Recent studies show that the Sunday school class is a small group that can be one of the more effective instruments for growth in understanding and discipleship. It offers fellowship. It provides information. It is no accident that Jesus chose twelve apostles. They experienced a special closeness to him and to one another.

I attended a meeting of religious educators and heard a speaker remind us that the Sunday school has great advantages: lay-led, innovative, oriented to personal commitment, the mainstay of funds for missions. Your search for faith, your effort to be strengthened in your personal beliefs, your effort to clarify your own position will be helped by participation in a study such as a Sunday school class.

An article in the *United Methodist Reporter* (October 31, 1986) was titled "Loving churches are growing churches, research shows." The article said that congregations searching for ways to attract members should concentrate less on traditional selling points such as church appearance, leadership, theology, and location but focus instead on how well they love. Research has found a correlation between an entire denomination's "love ability" (concern for each person) and its membership growth. What takes place during Sunday worship services to make people feel loved and cared for? Intercessory prayers? Sharing of joys and concerns? "Passing the peace" or an informal time to greet each other? How faithfully do members respond to known crises among fellow church members? Do members—and not just the pastor—make visits to hospitals and homes? These are questions the church might ask as it endeavors to make disciples. The primary task of the church is to reach out and receive people as they are, help them relate to God and strengthen that relationship, and then send them out to make their communities more loving and just. In other words, discipleship includes right thinking, sound theology, but it won't happen without the gathered community which we call the church. On one occasion I was asked to write an article for young adults around the question: "Is it possible to be a Christian and not belong to the church?" My answer was: "Of course." There is nothing in the New Testament that explicitly says you must belong to the church in order to be a Christian disciple. But I also said a person would not continue as a Christian very long without participation in the community of faith.

CHAPTER TWO
DISTINCTIVE EMPHASES OF THE WESLEYAN MESSAGE

he Methodist Church is more than The United Methodist Church. Worldwide, there are some sixty denominations that trace a spiritual ancestry to the Wesleys. These denominations are found in over ninety nations and encompass a constituency of about fifty million! While the United Methodist is the largest, it is only one among many. As we look at our own history here in the United States, it has been said that during the first fifty years our major emphasis was on evangelism. The growth of Methodism in the early nineteenth century is one of the remarkable chapters in church history. The second fifty years found a focus on education. Even today there are more than one hundred colleges, universities, and seminaries affiliated with our denomination.

The third fifty years emphasized missions. It's because of the outreach of persons such as a John R. Mott, who had a dream that the world should be evangelized in his generation, that Methodism is found in more than ninety different nations. In the last fifty years we have struggled to be faithful in uniting our religious experience with good works. There has been an emphasis on social concerns. There are four themes or emphases that characterize the Wesleyan message for today.

The first theme is *Catholic Spirit*. That is the title of a sermon preached by John Wesley. In the sermon—and we remember that he was speaking and writing before the days of inclusive language—he says, "A Methodist is solidly fixed in his religious principles, firmly adheres to that form of worship which he deems to be most acceptable, is united to a particular congregation, but his heart is open to all. That we call catholic or universal love." The notion of catholic spirit was incorporated by Wesley into the invitation to Holy Communion. It reads: "Ye that are in love and charity with your neighbors and intend to lead a new life following the commandments of God, draw near with faith." The denomination label is not a qualification for coming to Holy Communion. The only necessary commitment is that the communicant have faith in Christ and is seeking to be in love and charity with neighbors.

Methodists have always been people of catholic spirit! To ask the church (as some have) to withdraw from the National Council of Churches or the World Council of Churches would seek to deny our heritage. Participation in these conciliar movements does not mean that we agree on all matters, or that each individual endorses every resolution that is passed. It does mean that we have more in common than those things that separate us, and that it is important that we stand together in facing the dehumanizing forces of our secular world.

Martin Marty of the University of Chicago has written a book which he titled *The Public Church*. He says religion tends to organize itself into one of four categories: The Totalist (you can think of illustrations of those who insist on mind control); the Tribalist (those who affirm they alone have the truth and all others are in error); the Privatist (a growing phenomenon with the emergence of the electronic church). The fourth category he calls the Public Church. He says that mainline Protestantism, going clear back to George White-field, has always been concerned about the commonwealth. E. Stanley Jones once said that "all who name the name of Christ must be in conversation with everyone else who names the name of Christ." United Methodists are people of "catholic spirit." We are committed to ecumenism.

The second theme from Wesley is an acknowledgment that *"the world is my parish."* Our present temptation is to say "my parish is the world." Wesley was an ordained clergyman in the Church of England. As the Methodist movement began, however, the churches in

England were closed to him. His followers tended to be too enthusiastic for the established church. As a result, in response to an invitation by George Whitefield, he began preaching in the open air. The bishop of Bristol issued an order that forbade him to preach in the out-of-doors, and Wesley in a famed response replied that the world was his parish. We continue this emphasis.

The world is your parish when you are sensitive to hurts and concerns wherever they are found. John Wesley demonstrates this compassion through his mission to the American continent. We will continue in mission and evangelism.

Walbert Buhlman, a Jesuit research scholar, has written a book which he titled *The Third Church*. The first church was positioned in the Mediterranean basin, the second church was in Europe and later included the United States. The third church is found primarily in Africa, Asia, South America, and by the year 2000 will include a billion constituents, while in the West the church will only have 700 million. The child has become larger than the parent. We must continue with concern for the Third World. It will require that we understand the causes of some of the events taking place.

One of the United Methodist Bishops in the Philippians tells me why they had a change in government. Five percent of the population controlled 80 percent of the resources of the nation. The seeds of revolution are sown wherever such inequities exist. Many of us know that a revolution took place in Nicaragua in part because seventeen families controlled more than 90 percent of the nation's resources. Similar imbalances exist elsewhere in Latin America.

One business leader, who heads an organization that advises multi-national corporations, said (at a Futuring Consultation) that he told his clients to leave Iran almost three years before the Revolution. He discovered that the top 10 percent of the nation was receiving thirty-nine times as much as the bottom 10 percent. In an unstable culture he saw that condition would result in revolution. One of the most natural urges in the world is the desire for a better way of life. We must identify and empathize with that desire. Every day there are more persons who have not heard the story of Christ than the day before. The task is not finished. We combine a concern for justice and equity along with the fulfillment of the Great Commission to tell the story of Jesus Christ. The world *is* our parish. I am reminded of Wesley's approach to evangelism by the publisher of a newspaper, who talked with the Council of Bishops about how to use and also collaborate with the media. This person, who used to be a parishioner of mine in Cincinnati, told a story about his early childhood. He was reared in Southern Ohio where his father had been the school superintendent. He said he grew up with the idea that the role of the church was to make the world a better place in which to live. Then, he said, "When I grew old enough and had made enough money so that I could join the Chamber of Commerce, I discovered *they* thought it was *their* task!" He added, "I know now that the role of the church is indeed to make the world a better place in which to live, but its basic purpose is to bring men and women to the foot of the cross." Justice issues and evangelism should be united in one common purpose.

Third, Wesley, on one occasion, said that we must *"unite the two so long separated—knowledge and vital piety."* Most of the early clergy who spread the Methodist message were lay preachers. Many of the resources developed by Wesley were for the education of these persons. He also wanted to spread knowledge through the establishment of schools. But Wesley knew that knowledge separated from vital piety could be demonic. In his day the Anglican clergy of England constituted one of the better educated segments of society, but generally their lives were nonproductive because there was little vital piety. They were going through the routines of religious practice, but the nation was not being reformed, and persons were not being brought to a saving knowledge of Jesus Christ. Knowledge, of itself, is not enough.

Piety can be, of course, a negative word. Few of us would want to be known as pious. From misuse it offers a suggestion of that which is dour. That is why Wesley insisted there must be some vitality in it. So he spoke of the warmed heart, the joy of the Lord, of excitement and enthusiasm. He was not a worldling whose life needed correction. He was not an atheist who needed to be convinced about the truth of Christianity. His hand had long been in the service of Christ. But at Aldersgate his heart joined his head and his hand. What he had known theologically and practiced morally, he now apprehended experientially. There must be vitality, joy, and deep sense of commitment in the practice of our religion.

The final characteristic of our message is suggested by the Wesleyan phrase *Christian perfection.* Many of us grew up in an environment where we heard sermons about scriptural holiness, Christian perfection, sanctification, and the second blessing. Much of what Wesley taught on this matter, which he learned from the mystics and John Fletcher, has subsequently received further expression in twentieth-century Pentecostalism. The scholars do not agree on what he was trying to teach. I think one point, however, emerges quite clearly. He was calling Methodist people to disciplined living, to holy living. Our lives must be different from the lives of those who are in the secular world. He saw the spiritual dryness of the Anglican clergy. He was concerned that there seemed to be little difference between those who were in the church and those who were not. One historian reminds us that the philosophical mood in his day was rationalistic deism— that is, God had erected the world but then was gone. There was no personal relationship with God. The theological mood was a rigid kind of Calvinism. There was no grace in it. It was legalistic. The moral mood was profligate and degenerate. The entertainment stage in Wesley's day would equal ours in some of its excesses. The call to Christian perfection was a reminder that we are on a faith pilgrimage that includes holy and disciplined living.

At Annual Conference, candidates for ordination and membership are asked the historic questions designed by Wesley himself. One of these is, "Are you going on to perfection?" I have noted that when this question is asked, the ordinands often avert their eyes, shuffle their feet, and mumble. But then what would any of us say to such a question? It seems so utterly impossible. But the questioning, as it continues, becomes even more difficult. Next, "Do you expect to be made perfect in love in this life?" The first question implies a human effort to improve the quality of the life that we live. It suggests our striving to reach high moral standards. The second suggests that God does something within us, empowering us to do that which in our own human strength we cannot accomplish. The implication of these questions is clear. It was Wesley's intent that the clergy and laity live lives that were disciplined and holy, that we stand apart from the standards of the secular world by going on to perfection with integrity.

Carlyle Marney tells the story of General Dean who was captured in the Korean War. One morning his captors told him that in thirty minutes he would be executed. He was informed that if he wished to write a letter to his family he might do so. He had every moral reason to believe that what they said was actually going to take place. He was not executed, but his letter, written while he assumed he would be, has become a classic. It's only eight or nine lines in length, directed toward his wife, but right in the middle there is reference to their son, Bill. The oft-quoted sentence is this: "Tell Bill the word is integrity."

Not everyone agrees as to the meaning of this word *integrity*. Warren Bennis, a consultant to large corporations, in writing about the importance of morality in business, says: "By integrity I mean those standards of moral and intellectual honesty on which we base our lives, and from which we cannot swerve without cheapening ourselves." If the secular world expects that standard from its leaders, it is obvious that those who are followers of Christ must also demonstrate a standard of holiness that sets us apart from those who live by what is expedient.

The biography of Mary Bethune (1875-1955) illustrates a life of holiness with integrity. Her parents had been slaves. She attended a small, one-room segregated school in South Carolina. Arrangements were made for her to continue her studies at Moody Bible Institute in Chicago. She returned to South Carolina to teach. She had a dream. She had a vision that she would start a college. She went to Florida. She recruited five students and supported them by baking and selling pies. One of her customers was a Mr. Gamble. She recruited him to be the first chairman of her Board of Trustees. He was then involved in starting a soap factory in Cincinnati. (This in time became one of the leading firms in the nation—the Proctor and Gamble Company.)

Mary Bethune went on to become a national leader. She filled several responsible roles in the administration of Franklin Delano Roosevelt. There is a statue of her in Washington, D. C., and Bethune-Cookman College in Florida is named after her. She developed a remarkable ability to inspire and motivate young people. A line out of one of her commencement addresses reads: "Walk bravely in the light." (When you consider this was spoken before the Civil Rights struggle of the sixties, you realize how she spoke openly with integrity). "Faith ought not to be a puny thing. If you believe, believe like a giant, and may God grant you not peace, but glory."

United Methodists are a people who belong to a world parish. We are a people who have experienced the joy of the Lord. We are the people of catholic spirit. We are a people who bring dedicated and disciplined lives to our discipleship.

I hope these four emphases of the Wesleyan message will help you discover your discipleship among a people called United Methodist!

I gazed toward heaven in vision clear,
and watched the angel tall who waits to welcome
those whom God draws nigh the city with the twelve
white gates.
I spoke to him.
What strong soul led to Jesus caused this bright array?
His smile broke glorious as he said,
A man named Wesley passed this way.

Anonymous

CHAPTER THREE

GOD

 he statement on Doctrine, carried in the *1984 Discipline* of The United Methodist Church affirms that all valid Christian doctrine is born from our response in faith to the wondrous mystery of God's love in Jesus Christ as recorded in scripture. With all other Christian bodies we acknowledge belief in the triune God—Father, Son, and Holy Spirit. The statement also reminds us that the theological substance of our heritage begins with the biblical witness to God's reality as Creator and to God's gracious self-involvement in the dramas of history. We shall examine that "gracious self-involvement in the dramas of history" in the chapters on Jesus Christ and the Holy Spirit. In this chapter we begin with a consideration of our most basic belief, which is that of God as Creator.

Barriers

Rarely has there been a century when more questions are raised about faith in God. A phrase widely heard some years ago was *Christian Atheism*. This meant that you accepted the life and teachings of Jesus, and were inspired by them, but it was impossible to say that God existed. One professor wrote that the idea of God is too exalted for the concept of existence to apply. But looked at in the cold light of day, and stripped of all ambiguities, this kind of talk is really atheism and should be so identified.

A second barrier to belief is the position of anti-supernaturalism. You will remember the phenomenally popular book *Honest to God*. The author began by trying to debunk the idea of "God out there," for there is no triple-decker universe which the ancients described. Now we realize that if he were right, God is limited to the natural order and to whatever is in human experience. The author was not saying that he did not believe in God, but that he did not believe in God in a supernatural sense.

The problem is the ancient one of inward and outward—immanence and transcendence. By immanence we mean the indwelling of the divine world; by transcendence we mean that the divine reality is not limited to our natural order. Historically, basic Christianity has stressed both immanence and transcendence, but confusion has come in our time by the virtual denial of transcendence. The person who believes that God is merely "in here" is departing significantly from the witness of Christ, who in his most personal prayer addressed God as "Lord of Heaven and Earth," thus including both sides of the divine character.

The third major attack on the specifically Christian conception of God in our generation has been that of impersonalism. Christ, we know, approached the Father in a thoroughly personal fashion, especially in his prayers. But many contemporary men and women have been convinced that they cannot, with intellectual respectability, follow Christ in this regard. The chief instrument of their denial has been a use of the word *anthropomorphic,* which merely means "after the fashion of a man." Some people are told that if they employ the metaphor "father" and think of God as a person, they are falling back into primitive ways. When we say that God is a person, someone is likely to ask, "Do you really believe God is a big man up in the sky?" We must remember, however, that the only genuine alternative to "personal" is "impersonal." If God is nothing but "Life Force," "Eternal Values," or "Moral Law," we have cut the nerve of vital faith.

Some of the questions raised by the theological inquiry of recent years were necessary and helpful. When we heard the phrase, "God is dead," we realized that some of our notions about God were inadequate and should be allowed to die. Many were forced to recognize that God no longer existed as a Living Reality in their lives. The late Dr. Harold Bosley was taking part in a meeting of the World Council of Churches. He was interviewed by a reporter and Dr. Bosley assumed he would ask what the Council was going to say about some pressing world problem. But the reporter asked about the "death of God" by saying, "Is God really dead?" And Dr. Bosley asked, "What difference would it make to you, personally, this very minute if I should answer, Yes, God is dead?" The reporter changed the subject. For him, however, it was apparent that God was dead.

The need for sexually inclusive language has helped us see that there are many suitable metaphors which speak of God's personal relations with us. Most of us, however, find our faith in the existence of God shaken not by radical theologians but by the hard facts of life. There was the young woman who said, "I've watched four members of my family die with cancer. Surely you don't expect me to believe in a personal God who loves us and cares for us!" One can understand Hugh Walpole making a young man in one of his novels exclaim, "You know there can't be a God, Vanessa. In your heart you must know it. You are a wise woman. You read and think. Well, ask yourself, 'How can there be a God and life be as it is?' " Echoing this sentiment was the young university professor who commented, "I can't believe in God, although I sometimes wish I did." He is representative of a vast number who are troubled, feel doubt and confusion, are often inclined to resist the declarations of the church, and yet basically yearn for a vital faith.

Lord of Creation and History

We might profit from an examination of what we mean by a belief in "God's reality as Creator" and "God's gracious self-involvement in the dramas of history."

Consider, for a moment, the traditional arguments for the existence of God. There is the argument from cause and effect. Every effect must have its cause. There is the argument from life. We can alter, develop, rearrange, but we cannot create life. We transmit it, but life is a gift. If it is a gift, then this implies a giver. There is the argument from design. When we discover a world where there is order, where tides ebb and flow, and where the planets never leave their courses, we are bound to say: "I have found a world. Somewhere there must be a world-maker." There is the moral argument. The very word *ought* implies a standard given from beyond the human situation, and sanctions imposed by a power above. Then some find credence in the idea of the universal belief in God. There has never been discovered a tribe of men and women who did not pray.

Finally, there is the argument of experience. Through the centuries men and women of the highest reputation and of the strongest character have been convinced that in this universe there is a power other than human power. They base this conviction on the reality of their own experience. They are quite sure that God spoke to them in guidance and comfort, and in looking back they are confident they can trace the guiding hand of God. They would say that the presence of God is the most real thing in the world. There are those, however, who do not find these arguments conclusive.

A young graduate student said that in college he came in contact with a picture of the universe that was much more convincing than the Bible. It was, he said, built on real knowledge, on facts that have been tested scientifically. We make no claim for the biblical traditions of creation as scientific documents. It is abundantly clear that the writers of the creation story in Genesis were not interested in *When* and *What* and *How* but *Who* and *Why*.

The study of science is a proper task for us. God created us with curiosity. We seek answers. We want to know how things happened. However, remember that science is not the only avenue to truth. It is neutral and deals with very limited aspects of reality. Furthermore, the confirmed generalizations of all sciences admit that there need be no conflict between the sciences and a belief in a personal God, as some would suggest. We do not attack science; we are grateful for its contribution. But we do expect humility from scientists, for their field is not the final arbiter of truth. When we hear someone say, in referring to the biblical account of creation, "It couldn't have happened that way," or, "I don't believe in miracles," then we suspect that they are making judgments which are outside their scientific data.

A science magazine carried an important debate by reputable authorities on how the earth got here and where humankind came from. The conclusion: "We don't know. We have a lot of interesting theories—but we don't know." A few school systems are experimenting with the use of optional materials in talking about creation—including the Bible. At a meeting of the American Association for the Advancement of Science, John Moore, a professor of natural science at Michigan State, read a paper charging that evolution is a "religion" but not a science: "It is worth discussion and investigation," he said, "but more and more the results of disciplined experimentation fail to conform to what would be expected if Darwinism were true."

It is not our wish, however, to engage in the old debate of science versus revelation. Our purpose is to proclaim those basic beliefs which grasp us as United Methodists. And we are, in the first place, persuaded by tradition and reason that an orderly world affirms a Creator.

Our lives depend upon a dependable world. We measure our lives by the regular movement of the sun and the earth on which we live. The stability of our buildings, the power of our atomic energy, and the speed of our planes are all expressions of the regularity in the nature of things.

Now how did this orderly world get here? It didn't happen by chance. We know in our own lives that when anything is orderly and dependable, behind it is an engineering mind. The trustworthy, reliable operations of our world, our technology, are utterly dependent upon the order imposed by and utilized by the creative, ordering minds of men and women. On the basis of our experience, we must know that the presence of dependability in the universe implies the operation of an ordering principle.

W. McFerrin Stowe relates that scientist A. Cressy Morrison, in a simple illustration, has shown the improbability of chance in a universe of such perplexity. If you were to place ten coins in your pocket, numbered one through ten, the chance of drawing them out in succession would be one in ten billion. He concludes: "So many essential conditions are necessary for life to exist on our earth that it is impossible that all of them could exist in proper relationship by chance. Therefore, there must be in nature some form of intelligent direction."

Furthermore, Mr. Morrison has pointed out that the earth is tilted at 23.5 degrees. If it were tilted more or less, life as we know it could not exist—but it is tilted exactly at 23.5 degrees. What a mind it took to plan the earth so there would be daylight and dark, land and sea, summer and winter, seedtime and harvest, animals and plants, rain and sunshine.

Our world is full of wonders that defy any rational explanation and call for the presence of a great and all-powerful Creative Mind. Consider the story of the monarch butterflies. These tiny, fragile members of God's creation, weighing little more than a bird's feather, fly hundreds of miles to spend the winter in warmer climates. The flocks of butterflies that span the North American continent and arrive in late October at Pacific Grove, California, have long been famous. An estimated two million monarchs spend the winter, year after year, on the same trees in a six-acre area. The most spectacular feature of their migration is that they gather on these same trees each year. Their life span is so short, no butterfly could possibly make the round trip twice. How then, do they find their way over such great distances? There is only one answer: God has provided compass and direction!

Observe the care with which the mother wasp provides for her children. When the mother wasp has laid her eggs, she stings a grasshopper in exactly the right spot so that he does not die but is completely paralyzed, living as a kind of preserved meat. She then drags the grasshopper to where the eggs are, flies away and dies, never setting eyes on her eggs again. When the eggs finally hatch, the baby wasps have their food supply in the form of instant grasshopper right at hand. Now, all this is an enormously complicated process; there is no margin for error, and the first mother wasp who set this process in motion had to do it perfectly, or today there would be no wasps.

As you reflect upon this, you realize that the mother wasp has been endowed with a marvelous set of instincts to take care of her children. You reason back from these instincts to the creative force in the universe, and you conclude that the wasp—and indeed, the whole natural order—must be the work of a Supreme Intelligence.

These incidents out of nature illustrate the need for an organizing intelligence which stands both above and within this universe. Dr. Robert Jasrow gave a series of television lectures on "The New Science." He used the word *accident* a number of times. "Various stages of development," he said, "were the result of an accident—a happenstance." This is as difficult to accept intellectually as the biblical notion of six days! God is a God of order. Chaos is anti-God!

The second affirmation, however, is more difficult. The Christian faith proclaims that this Creative Impulse is aware of itself, is a person. Again, we must base our convictions not only upon the scripture but also upon our own experience.

In this world, we say, persons are distinct in that they are aware, examine, and try to understand themselves. If persons are self-aware, then the ultimate nature of reality must include the personal. Chester Pennington illustrates this in the following way: When a wife brings chocolate cake to the dinner table, remarking that she baked it from scratch, we must assume that in the universe which produced it (her kitchen) there existed the ingredient of chocolate. It cannot appear if it does not exist. So when self-awareness appears in persons, it must have already existed. That which is highest in ourselves is a reflection of that which is deepest in the universe!

In other words, as human intelligence implies the existence of intelligence in the very nature of things, so human personality implies the existence of personality at the very core of reality. We are moved to conclude that not only is there a Creative Intelligence in this universe, but this Organizing Power is a Person with self-awareness. In this sense, while God and humanity belong to two utterly different orders, there is an affinity between them which was brought about by God. You and God both have self-awareness and are both persons!

The third affirmation held by United Methodists about God is that while God is beyond humanity, God is also for us. God is for us because we are created in the divine image (Genesis 1:27). The earliest historian of note in the British Isles was the venerable Bede. It was he who wrote of a man who described life as the flight of a sparrow out of darkness across a lighted banquet hall into darkness. Many might find this an apt description. They would have difficulty with Wordsworth's idea expressed in his ode on "Intimations of Immortality" when he wrote: "But trailing clouds of glory do we come, from God, who is our home." We believe that God created humankind out of the divine nature for a purpose. God does not despise but cherishes what is made in God's own image.

In the divine relationship with the creatures and humanity, God has accepted two limitations. God is limited by the structure of creation. If this world is to be reasonable and intelligent, then it must be subject to the orderliness to which we have referred. I must not expect God to periodically intervene and upset the natural course of events in my behalf. If God were to do that, even once, then the Creator could be guilty of being capricious, of saving some and not others.

We often assume that if God is love, there will be a discriminatory power exercised for us. We do not want God to make the sun to rise on the just and the unjust but to reserve it for the just. We plead, "Why did this happen to me? I go to church every Sunday?" Does this mean that the laws of aging in which vital human organs wear out should not apply to us? Does this mean that the laws of this universe are to be set aside for us so that if we fall we are not injured as others? Eighty-seven children and three teachers were killed in a parochial school fire. In a television interview following the tragedy, a clergyman called it "the will of God." What a frightful thing to say. If God plots such tragedies, why should we bother with building codes, safety regulations, and fire escapes? And why bother with God?

Leslie Weatherhead, in his helpful volume on the will of God, tells of visiting a friend in India during an epidemic. The friend's son died. The two men were walking on the veranda of the home. At the far end of the porch a tiny girl, the only remaining child, lay asleep under a mosquito net. The father said, "Well, Reverend, it's the will of God."

Knowing the man intimately, and wanting to help him think through the implications of this comment, Weatherhead replied, "Suppose someone crept up the steps onto the veranda tonight while you all slept, and deliberately put a wad of cotton soaked in cholera germ culture over your little girl's mouth as she lay there . . . what would you think about that?"

"My God," the father cried, "I'd kill him with as little feeling as I would a snake."

"But John," Weatherhead said, "isn't that just what you've accused God of doing when you said it was his will? Call your little boy's death the result of mass ignorance, call it mass folly, call it mass sin . . . but don't call it the will of God."

This point of view may raise questions as to the meaning of intercessory prayer. A later discussion will consider this matter. The only point we are now trying to make is that God has created a dependable universe. The Christian is as subject to the laws of this world as the next person. Prayer is concerned with matters other than trying to get God to do what God ordinarily would not do.

God also chooses to be limited by the reality of human freedom. We are not automatons. We have been set free in this world so that through joy and sorrow, success and failure, we are free to become genuine persons, molding our own lives. Often it is asked why God allows people to make war, to build slums, and to create the injustices that abound. But to ask why God does not stop war, or why God allows exploitations and slums, is to ask why God does not stop being God. Because the Creator is a God of love, we creatures will not be treated as less than free human beings, who must learn and grow and come at last to travail perhaps, but who will be spiritual personalities rather than automatic machines.

Jesus told a matchless story in which he said God is like a father. A father does not shut us in a room away from danger. He permits us to mature through experience, to use our freedom even though it carries a risk. And a real father, while he may not always be able to keep us from danger, suffers with us while we go through the difficult experience. For the Christian, this is part of the meaning of Christ, who "reflects the glory of God and bears the very stamp of his nature . . ." (Hebrews 1:3).

In spite of these limitations which God willingly assumes, we still affirm that God is *for* us, and loves us with an everlasting love. A former governor of Wyoming, Milward Simpson, in a devotional article, tells of flying in a plane that developed trouble. When the pilot announced they were going to try an unscheduled emergency landing, the governor took the hand of his wife, and together they offered a simple statement of faith they often shared:

> The light of God surrounds us,
> The love of God enfolds us,
> The power of God protects us,
> And the presence of God watches over us;
> Wherever we are, God is.

Then he added that they knew the asserting of this affirmation would not make everything turn out all right. Rather, saying what they said was their way of declaring the confidence that "living or dying, we are in his care." This is what we mean when we say, "God is *for* us."

A young woman came to her pastor with a question, "How can I believe that God is interested in what happens to me?"

The pastor answered, "Look at your fingers. There are billions of fingertips in the world, but no others are like yours. Even your fingertips have had special attention from God." Then she was instructed, "Whenever you doubt, look at your handcarved fingertips and know that God is interested in you personally."

In this chapter we have been talking about our faith in God, the source of life, the One in whom we live, move, and have our being. It is well that we remember God's greatness. At the funeral of Louis XIV, the cathedral was filled with mourners who had come to pay their final tribute to the King, whom they all considered to be great. The room was dark, save for one lone candle illuminating the gold casket which held the mortal remains of the monarch. At the appointed time, the Court Preacher stood to address the citizens. As he rose he reached from his pulpit and snuffed out the one candle which had been put there alone to symbolize the greatness of the King. Then from the darkness came just four words, "God only is great."

CHAPTER FOUR

CHRIST

he Doctrinal Statement of our General Conference recognized that the ecumenical process has expanded across the boundaries of Christian unity, to include serious interfaith encounters and explorations between Christianity and other living religions of the world. We must now be conscious that God has been and is now working among all people. There is a new sense in which we realize that we are given to each other on this fragile small planet, to work out with God the salvation, health, healing, and peace intended for all people. In these less familiar encounters, however, our aims are not to reduce doctrinal differences to some lowest common denominator or religious agreement, but to raise all such relationships to the highest possible level of human fellowship and understanding.

A Unique Christ

We are Christians because we believe there is something distinctive about Christianity. We are persuaded that in the midst of our condition of need and alienation, God's unfailing grace shows itself in his suffering love working for our redemption and that the Gospels describe this fact in a way that is not recorded elsewhere.

United Methodists believe we have a faith of incomparable power and beauty which we should cherish and increasingly understand. Many in our own household, however, view it as commonplace. Intrigued by tantalizing reports of foreign faiths, some of our own youth are going to India to meditate under the guidance of a Guru, or they turn to such mystical religions as Zen Buddhism for satisfaction. For their sake, and to engage meaningfully in interfaith dialogue, we must be prepared to answer the question, "Why Christianity of all religions?"

We speak from a stance of humility. We acknowledge that most of us are what we are because of birth. Furthermore, in contemporary missions the approach is dialogical. The missionary does not come in arrogance saying, "I have the truth, and I will now share it with you who are benighted." He or she says, "I have something to learn; I have something to offer."

Nevertheless, there are two assumptions we must reject. Under the guise of tolerance we sometimes say: "All religions are equally true. It doesn't make any difference what you believe as long as you are sincere." A scientist would never say that. If you go to a doctor, you want from him or her more than sincerity. An engineer would not say that. If you board an airplane, you want the pilot not only to be sincere but to know there are some laws in nature you do not violate with impunity.

In our modern culture we have exalted to an astonishing degree the conception of broadmindedness. In the area of religion, this finds expression in the claim that Christianity is only one of several great world religions, and Jesus Christ is only one of a number of great religious teachers. We must reject this misconceived tolerance. All religions are not equally true. Some of the most dastardly acts of human history have been perpetrated in the name of religion! In the name of religion, widows have been killed and buried with their husbands. In the name of religion, a devout mother in India has been known to take her cherished child to the Ganges River and throw him into the water as a sacrifice to the gods. In the name of religion, some of our forebears in New England destroyed certain members of the community because they were suspected of being witches. The hearty relativism that one person's religion is as good as another person's is fuzzy thinking and does not stand up before the facts.

Another misconception is found in the phrase: "We're all going to the same place; we're just taking different roads." This phrase is acceptable if it means that denominational labels are not very important. The proposition, however, that all the major world religions are so many different ways to the same goal breaks down before the facts. The Buddhist believes that the thirst for life, the desire for this unreal world, gives rise to suffering. The Buddhist's goal is to find the way to Nirvana, which is total discontinuance or extinction. Followers of

Mohammed may have as their goal the joys of paradise where they can enjoy to the full the sensuous delights of the flesh. In Christianity our goal is to be set free from the power of sin, from bondage to the powers which rule over us from within so that we are able to give ourselves to the true service of God, for in obedience we find our highest joy. Tolerance, unfortunately, is often another name for indifference. Neutrality usually means spiritual and mental paralysis. We reject these even as we search for real communication among the world religions.

Why Christianity? Because it offers us a God who is "Love." We have heard this phrase so often that it has been worn smooth. For most of the world, however, it comes with the force of a fresh revelation. The power of these words can be understood only when we trace the history of humankind's religious endeavors and find that most of our efforts have been directed toward placating an angry, vindictive, capricious God!

In Westminster Abbey there is a plaque marking the burial place of David Livingstone, immortal missionary of another generation. He was attacked by wild beasts, buried his wife in the jungle, and died on his knees by his cot in Africa. His body was then carried with honor to Westminster Abbey where he lies with kings and queens. It is said that at his funeral they sang his favorite hymn which has in it this line:

> O God of Bethel, by whose hand
> Thy people still are fed. . . .

Through all the vicissitudes of his life he never doubted but that God's sovereign purpose for him was created out of love. This vibrant note runs through the entire Judaeo-Christian witness from the Twenty-Third Psalm with its assurance that "The Lord Is My Shepherd. . . . " to the Book of Revelation with these comforting words: "Behold, the dwelling of God is with (people). . . . (God) will wipe away every tear from their eyes, and death shall be no more, neither shall there be mourning nor crying nor pain any more, for the former things have passed away" (Revelation 21:3-4). The philosopher's question is asked in these terms, "Is the universe friendly?" to which the Christian affirms, "God is love."

Eddie Cantor, who was brought up in the slums of New York City's East Side, tells in his autobiography how one summer as a youngster he was scooped off the hot and dirty streets and taken to a summer camp along the cool and refreshing Hudson River. For the first time in his memory he had three good meals every day. One night he got to wondering how he happened to be there, why it wasn't costing anything. Another kid in the tent had the answer. "Because somebody's interested in kids like us." Eddie went to sleep that night murmuring to himself, "Thank you, somebody." And then adds, "That was the closest I ever got to religion in those days." This is what Christianity affirms. Somebody's interested in folks like us. We are not in this world alone. God has expressed himself as love.

In the second place, we believe Christianity is unique in offering us a leader who was and is as "no other man." Our doctrinal statement reminds us that "at the heart of the gospel of salvation is God's self-presentation in Jesus of Nazareth. . . . In his life we see the power and wisdom of God, confirming his new covenant with his people in the revelation of the fullness of human possibilities." What is Christian? Is a person a Christian simply by virtue of not being a Muslim or a Buddhist or a Jew? If so, a criminal might justifiably wear the Christian label. Are we Christian simply because we live according to the Golden Rule? Any decent and respectable agnostic may fulfill that condition.

A Personal Christ

To find an answer we must go back to the beginning and remember that, when Jesus walked beside the Sea of Galilee, there was not another Christian in the world. Peter, Andrew, James, and John were good men who feared God and kept the law, but they could not properly be called Christians. These four fishermen became Christians only on a day when Jesus said, "Follow me," and they forsook their nets and followed him. So we have our answer. A Christian is someone who responds to the call of Christ. First and always, Christianity is a relationship to a Person. In that sense it differs from the world religions like Judaism and Hinduism and all rival faiths that compete for men's and women's allegiance. All these direct our loyalty to a theological system, a code of ethics, a philosophy, or an ideology, but Christianity alone directs our loyalty to a Person. Where Christ is, there is Christianity, and the Christian is a person who tries to be a follower of Jesus Christ.

A leader sets an example. The attack on Pearl Harbor was led by Captain Fuchida. Later in the war, when General Doolittle carried out his famous raid on Tokyo, one of the American men shot down was Sergeant Jacob De Shazer. He spent the rest of the war in a Japanese prison camp and received brutal treatment. After the war, he returned to the United States, entered seminary, and prepared himself to go to Japan as a missionary. There he and Captain Fuchida met. The Captain was puzzled as to why anyone would come back to Japan after what the Sergeant had gone through.

Then he met a young missionary woman, daughter of two missionaries who had been beheaded by the Japanese during the war. He found all this unbelievable. Why would these people want to spend their lives with their enemies? He secured a copy of the Bible to see what it was all about. When he came to that passage where Jesus, hanging on the cross, prays for his enemies saying, "Father, forgive them, for they know not what they do," he understood. Sergeant De Shazer and the young woman were doing what their leader had done.

Christ gave us an example, not only of how to accept hardship, but of how to live with enthusiasm and joy. The New Testament contains enough tragedy to make it the saddest book in the world, but it opens with the songs of angels bringing tidings of great joy, and it closes with the Hallelujah Chorus sung by all the ransomed hosts of heaven.

A young English clergyman, shortly after his ordination, crossed the Channel and visited Paris. When he returned, one of his friends asked if he had enjoyed Paris and he said, "Yes, but I wish I had visited it before I was converted." This is representative of what most people believe about religion. It is a negative, something which inhibits and represses. It "takes the fun out of living." We assert that there is not a single thing in this whole world to which we are not entitled if it will do us good and be profitable. Christianity is against drunkenness, because it is destructive. Christianity is against adultery, because it is a sickness. Christianity is against hate and revenge, because they erode spiritual potential. But everything that is life-fulfilling is ours to enjoy. Jesus lived life from a great depth of being and with joy! And we are to live this way.

Not only does a leader give an example to those who follow, but also believes in them and their potential for greatness. We are grateful for the Christian estimate of humanity as beings of infinite value and worth. The Christian doctrine of human nature conceives persons as bearing the image of God, as agents of moral discernment, as capable of making a faith response, and as having a personal responsibility for helping establish social structures of equity. Buddhism does not provide this understanding, and thoughtful Japanese leaders have expressed a concern as to how long democracy can prevail without a concept of persons as having unique and inherent dignity. Certainly the Hindu principle of Nirvana (which is final and total escape) cannot provide the impulse for transforming society. In Buddhism it is not transformation of reality but salvation from reality which is the basic attitude. In any religious moral code the basic question relates to the intrinsic aim of existence. Christianity emphasizes not only the fact of God but also brings the human person into focus as responsible for the "Fall," as one inevitably a sinner, but one who is also capable of a response of faith which results in a life committed to establishing the kingdom of God as the ultimate reality.

Christianity is not passive. It believes persons can do something about helping to fashion this unfinished creation. It believes each person can responsibly involve himself or herself. We are in the mainstream of Christian affirmation when we sing:

> Rise up, O men of God! Have done with lesser things;
> Give heart and mind and soul and strength
> To serve the King of Kings.
> Rise up, O men of God! His kingdom tarries long;
> Bring in the day of brotherhood
> And end the night of wrong.
>
> *Book of Hymns*, No. 174

A Perfect Christ

Christianity also has a uniqueness in that it lays upon us the call to perfection. It recognizes our weakness, but does not temper its claims and demands by our frailty. Again and again, in the Sermon on the Mount, Jesus lays upon his followers the burden of seemingly impossible moral and ethical ideals. Who can really love an enemy? Can we honestly pray for those who despitefully use us? Who can go on and on forgiving in the face of ingratitude? Who can ever measure up to the demand that Jesus phrased in the words, "You, therefore, must be perfect, even as your heavenly Father is perfect" (Matt. 5:48)?

The only way to spiritual growth is to reach for that which is always beyond our grasp. We must not become satisfied and fashion ideals to meet our accomplishments. The church must never be a reflection of the morals and ideals of its members. All of us feel there is more love to express, more truth to comprehend, more work to be accomplished. Christianity believes we can grow all our lives.

Some years ago there was a film about Red Nichols and his Five Pennies. This was the day of the big bands, and the Five Pennies included Glenn Miller, the Dorsey Brothers, and Artie Shaw. The joy of Red's life was his daughter who was stricken with polio. He traveled across a continent to be at her bedside. Much of the film was devoted to showing how he worked with his daughter. He kept pushing her beyond her grasp. When he brought a puppy home, he would place it on the hillside and let her climb and stretch and strain for it. Sometimes it seemed cruel to ask the impossible, but it was the only way she could regain the use of her legs. Growth is possible only as we strain and stretch, never arriving, never completely grasping, but always reaching for more knowledge, more understanding, more love, more of the mind of Christ.

The worth of an ideal is never measured merely by the degree to which we attain but by the direction it gives life. The flower, reaching for the sun, never reaches its goal except in responding to the upward pull; the dynamic of life and growth is within the flower. We may never in this lifetime attain all that is implied in the ideal, "You, therefore, must be perfect, even as your heavenly Father is perfect," but in reaching toward that we have within us the dynamic of growth. We are grateful for a religion and a faith that keeps expecting great things of us, that keeps us reaching and growing all of life. Paul said he did not count himself as having attained final growth, but he was pressing toward the mark.

There is one final thought. This principle of growth applies not only to this life but to the world to come. For the problem of sin and evil, there is the promise of forgiveness, salvation, and "eternal life." For the problem of suffering, there is the promise of increasing victory and the final weaving into a joyous pattern, although we may not fully understand until we have the perspective of eternity. For the problem of death, there is the promise of survival and reunion. We lift our eyes above the shadows of earth and see the light of eternity.

CHAPTER FIVE

HOLY SPIRIT

n the section on "Distinctive Emphases of
United Methodists" in the Doctrinal Statement there is this sentence: "One of the
most familiar accents in traditional United
Methodist teaching has been on the pri-
macy of grace. By grace we mean God's loving action in human
existence through the ever-present agency of the Holy Spirit." While
this is a distinctive emphasis, we United Methodists share with all
Christians in believing in the Holy Spirit. At times we have neglected
this doctrine, and we must acknowledge that we have often misunderstood it. But as Bishop Mack Stokes reminds us, "We have been
true to New Testament Christianity whenever we stressed the power
and presence of the Holy Spirit."

Three Persons

By having affirmed that as United Methodists we believe in the
Holy Spirit, we hasten to add that the Christian faith, contrary to
what is often assumed, does not have three distinct persons, separate
from each other, as God.

The late Cardinal Cushing told in an address to a group of Protestant clergy that when he was a parish priest he was summoned to a
store to give the last rites to a man who had collapsed. Following
the custom of his church, he knelt by the man and asked: "Do you
believe in God the Father, God the Son, and God the Holy Spirit?"
He said the man roused a little, opened one eye, looked at the
people standing around, and said: "Here I am dying, and he asks
me a riddle."

No doctrine is more misunderstood than the Christian concept of the Trinity. When we say "God in three persons, blessed Trinity," however, we are using the word *persons* in the sense in which the word *Persona* was used in the theater of classical Greece and Rome. It meant the mask, put on by actors, in order to play different parts. The word was taken over by early theologians to express the diverse forms of God's activity without destroying the concept of God's unity.

When we use the name, Holy Spirit, we are saying that we believe God can indwell, inspire, energize, and motivate men and women. We are saying that we believe God is expressed in beauty, truth, goodness, and love. We also believe that the Holy Spirit, as someone has phrased it, "is the unseen Presence rebuking us for every evil thought and deed, confirming us in every good thing, and summoning us to creative advances with God and humanity." The Doctrinal Statement reminds us that Grace (God's loving action in human existence through the ever-present agency of the Holy Spirit) is the spiritual climate and environment surrounding all human life at all times and in all places. "Prevenient grace" is the divine love that anticipates all our conscious impulses and that persuades the heart toward faith.

When we say Holy Spirit, we are thinking of the spiritual presence of Jesus of Galilee. Jesus promised, "I will not leave you desolate." And Paul wrote, "If any man have *not* the Spirit of Christ, he is none of his." Furthermore, when the Holy Spirit was poured out upon the disciples at Pentecost, they were convinced that Jesus was back in their midst as he had promised. The presence they experienced was not something strange but the reality of Christ in their midst once again.

The number three is incidental. We are simply saying that these are the ways we know God, and we are also saying that all these expressions are manifestations of the One God. We are *mono*-theistic, not *tri*-theistic. When we say, "God the Father, God the Son, and God the Holy Spirit," we are saying that we know God as Sovereign Creator; we know God as revealed in Jesus of Galilee; we know God as a Presence within us now for comfort and for strength.

If this still seems confused, and if the Holy Spirit seems elusive of definition, let's remember that since the human personality baffles the wisest psychologists of our day, we can hardly hope to do more than make guesses about the supra-personality of a Sovereign God.

Manifestations

It is appropriate, however, that we discover again this distinctive emphasis of our heritage. During this century, both the religious and the secular press carry periodic reports of a surging new spirit of religious fervor sweeping across the land. The major secular magazines have carried articles about the appearance of the glossolalia movement in the old-line churches, including the Roman Catholic. *Glossolalia* is a term transliterated from the Greek word for "tongue" or "language." The term refers mainly to the so-called "gifts," in 1 Corinthians 12:4. This is the incoherent speech of religious ecstasy. There are many who consider this a sign that the believer is possessed of the Holy Spirit. We should remember, however, that this phenomenon caused disorder in the Christian assembly at Corinth. Paul did not reject it outright, but he discussed the problems caused by this "gift" and advocated the principle that all must be done for edification. Since speaking in "tongues" does not conform to this principle, Paul placed prophecy above glossolalia in his list of "gifts of the Spirit."

In general, United Methodists acknowledge the right of an individual to express his or her devotional feelings in private through the ecstasy of "tongues" but have resisted the public manifestation. There are too many dangers associated with the movement to make it a central part of our emphasis or tradition. It has rarely been a part of the public worship service in United Methodism.

This does not mean, in the first place, that we are uninterested in the manifestation of the Holy Spirit in our personal and corporate lives. But the results we seek are more functional. Our Doctrinal Statement affirms that the Holy Spirit is the active cause of our justification, by which we are made new creatures in Christ. It is the agency of nurture by which the believers "grow in grace" and in Christian understanding. It is the instrument by which the Christian life is crowned with the perfection of love (sanctification). In this context, the New Testament exhortation that we be filled with the

Holy Spirit has found a wide reception, and the experience of Pentecost has been restored to its position as normative Christianity. For us, however, normative is not "speaking in tongues" but opening one's life to the Holy Spirit in such a way that the Spirit can signify God's acceptance and pardoning love, make us new creatures in Christ, perfect us in God's *agape* love, and thereby empower us for effective Christian witness. The baptism with the Spirit is a baptism of love and an empowerment for evangelism or witness.

Wesleyans have generally placed heavy stress on the ethical manifestations of the Spirit's presence. The New Testament sums up the doctrine in this phrase, "the spirit of Christ." To John the Baptist, God said, "He on whom you see the Spirit descend and remain, this is he who baptizes with the Holy Spirit" (John 1:33b). At his baptism Jesus was revealed as the Bearer of the Spirit. The descending dove marked him as the Anointed of God. Pentecost disclosed Jesus as the Spirit-Baptizer. In this event the Spirit of God became the Holy Spirit of our Lord Jesus Christ. He became the supreme manifestation, as the Spirit became the medium through whom Christ comes to indwell and sanctify his church. In other words, Christ is the pattern of the Spirit-filled life. The Holy Spirit is therefore the Christ-Spirit. It was not, however, until Jesus gave up his life forgivingly on the cross that that pattern was complete. "Christ also suffered for you, leaving you an example, that you should follow in his steps. . . . When he was reviled, he did not revile in return; when he suffered; he did not threaten; but he trusted to him who judges justly" (1 Pet. 2:21-23). The Spirit of Jesus is the "Spirit of the Cross." The spirituality recognized in the New Testament has an ethical dimension. When we have "the Spirit," we are Christlike in our suffering, forgiveness, compassion, and caring.

Thus the Christian experience of the Holy Spirit means, primarily, to have "Christ formed in us." When this happens we can say, "For me to live is Christ." Paul prays for God's people who are now the "dwelling place of God in the Spirit" (Eph. 2:22) that Christ may dwell in their hearts by faith. One translation renders this, "That Christ may make his home in your hearts." This is the same as being filled with all the fullness of God.

It was the spiritual genius of John Wesley that he saw that this sanctification (or perfection of love, as the Doctrinal Statement defines it) lies at the very heart of Christ's redemptive activity. One of Wesley's earliest Oxford sermons notes that "the title Holy applied to the Spirit of God does not only denote that he is holy in his own nature, but that he makes us so; that he is the great fountain of holiness to his church. The Holy Spirit is the principle of the conversion and entire sanctification of our lives." One scholar observes that "Wesleyan theology was preeminently a doctrine of the Holy Spirit." He was bearing witness to the New Testament truth that the Spirit of Christ is the sanctifying Spirit and that all his ministrations are to the end of making us holy and Christlike persons. Christian perfection was a life of such intimate communion with God, made possible through the sanctifying presence of the Holy Spirit, that the natural fruit of that relationship had ethical dimensions. "We were made perfect in love." The gifts of the Spirit are not "spiritual things" for personal aggrandizement. They are "grace gifts" which make us loving and humble like Jesus. They are those spiritual endowments which enable us to contribute to the common good of the Body of Christ. There are those who question whether a gift can be said to "exist" for the individual if it is not employed for the sake of building up the Body of Christ in loving unity.

Paul comes to the heights of New Testament truth when he says, "Now I will show you the best way of all, without which all other gifts are nothing." First Corinthians 13 is the way of *agape* love (love given in response to God's love for us, a response in which we give of ourselves in building up life). In *A Plain Account of Christian Perfection,* Wesley makes Paul's point clear: "Another ground of a thousand mistakes is, not considering deeply, that love is the highest gift of God; humble, gentle, patient love; that all visions, revelations manifestations whatever, are little things compared to love; and that all gifts are either the same with, or infinitely inferior to it."

Comforter

The gift of the Holy Spirit, bringing sanctification, has a practical and ethical result. We are made "perfect in love." There are, however, other dimensions. The Doctrinal Statement would remind us that "out of our heritage we gratefully reaffirm belief in 'Prevenient grace,' the divine love that anticipates all our conscious impulses and that persuades the heart toward faith. . . . He continues to nur-

ture the believers as they 'grow in grace' and in Christian understanding." Another way of saying this is found in one of the creeds
printed in the United Methodist *Book of Hymns* which says the Holy
Spirit is "God present with us for guidance, comfort, and strength."
   The first Christians, left desolate by Jesus' death, found, to their
immense joy and faith, that they were not comfortless. They had the
experience of Pentecost. They experienced a Presence which continued to comfort, sustain, inspire, and lead. Jesus had told his
disciples that he was going away. They felt lonely, fearful, and confused. Then he promised to send another Comforter. "And I will
pray the Father, and he shall give you another Comforter, that he
may abide with you forever" (John 14:16, KJV). The Greek word
translated "Comforter" is *paraclete*. It literally means "one called to
one's side." The Holy Spirit brings the God who is above us to our
side; the Spirit transposes the Jesus of history and makes him our
living contemporary. The God who is above us has come to us and
walks by us, dwells in us, in the person of the Holy Spirit. The
hymn writer says:

> Holy Spirit, faithful guide
> Ever near the Christian's side
> Gently lead us by the hand,
> Pilgrims in a desert land.
>
> *Book of Hymns*, No. 106

This comfort comes through prayerful waiting. We are often under
such pressure we don't give the Spirit a chance to work in us or
come to us. Jesus said, "Peace I leave with you; my peace I give to
you" (John 14:27). Repentance is also necessary as a prelude to receiving the Holy Spirit as Comforter. The Spirit working in us is
the "active cause of our justification, by which we are made new
creatures in Christ." Before this can happen, we must repent. Peter
was preaching and his listeners were cut to the quick. They cried,
"What must we do?" Peter answered, "Repent and be baptized in
the name of Jesus Christ, so that you may have your sins forgiven
and receive the gift of the Holy Spirit."
   The Holy Spirit is the agent of power in the Christian's life. The
instruction of Jesus to the disciples was to tarry until endued with
power. Life is easily lost in triviality, meaninglessness, and frustra-

tion. Human experience has demonstrated, however, that when we are touched and quickened by the Holy Spirit, we become valiant and can serve God as we could not do before.

The memory of Pentecost haunts us as we recall the power surging in the hearts of the disciples. Where is that power today? Can it come among us again? Undoubtedly we would wish to experience it in an altogether different and new way. We might not look for a dove or tongues of fire. The power we seek must accord with a realistic view of the world. It is the power to care about ourselves and one another and the world. Jesus did not come just to start a new branch of organized religion. His purpose was to redeem humankind, and it was with this purpose that the disciples were so vitally energized at Pentecost. We live in a revolutionary age, full of unrest among students, the blacks, the poor. Jesus was a revolutionary. He talked about faith moving mountains. The Holy Spirit is the source of power for Christians to get on with the task to which we have been commissioned and to use our personal and social resources in God's way! We must take this doctrine of the Holy Spirit seriously—not because it will restore the church (though that may happen as a by-product) but because only by becoming bearers of God's redeeming grace can we ourselves hope to be redeemed.

Guide

A further function of the Holy Spirit is to give guidance. The Bible is filled with illustrations: In the Old Testament God's will was made known through dreams, visions, and direct conversation. The Gospels tell us that Jesus was led of the Spirit, into the wilderness, back to Nazareth, and through his ministry. In Acts 16:6-10 we are told how the Apostle Paul was led by the Spirit to go to Macedonia and thus the gospel was brought to Europe for the first time. And in the first verse of the Book of Acts there is an interesting idea: Luke writes, "In the first book (the Gospel) . . . I have dealt with all that Jesus began to do and teach. . . . " He began, but didn't finish. In fact, he told his disciples that when he had gone from them the Spirit would come and lead them into all truth. In other words, the Bible is not a closed book. God kept on talking when the book had gone to press. God is a living God and there is truth and guidance for every follower. We are impressed by how many Christian people testify to the idea that they receive divine guidance and leadership when they seek it!

Even as we affirm the reality of divine guidance, we must test the Spirit! We may feel we have received guidance but we are not infallible. A woman said the Lord told her to leave her husband, but when the husband was consulted he said no such message had been given to him. John Wesley sometimes would let the Bible fall open and then would seize whatever verse his eye found as God speaking to him. I have also done this, but I accompany it with a prayer saying, "Lord, I need help; lead me to a biblical passage that speaks to my need." And it frequently happens. But often it does not. There is the old story of the man seeking help who opened the Bible and the verse he discovered was, "and Judas went and hanged himself." He didn't like that so he tried again and this time the verse was, "Go thou and do likewise."

There are few decisions that are irremediable when a mistake has been discovered. All does not hang on a single judgment. Persons who really believe in God count on the new initiative in life which God with men and women can always effect, thus they can approach things with a kind of "holy carelessness."

We need also to recognize our capacity for self-deception. We can easily deceive ourselves into thinking that what we want to do is right. (What may seem to be the Holy Spirit may be the devil of self-assertion.) A prison chaplain writes of a study in which he talked with twelve inmates in the penitentiary. He asked each, "Why are you here?" The answers were instructive: "I was framed." "They ganged up on me." "It was a case of mistaken identity." "The police had it in for me." Not one said he was guilty of something. They were all innocent. An insurance adjuster said that he would estimate 90 percent of the people involved in automobile accidents see themselves as blameless.

There are several ways by which the Holy Spirit guides us. Prayer is one, but this requires a spirit of genuine, unconditional obedience. Are we willing to take the answer we receive? If not, then we must not expect guidance. Don't expect answers to be dictated, but find a place where you can be quiet, unhurried, and wait. What we should do in prayer is think over the matter carefully in the presence of God, then pray for his guidance and light, asking that he call our attention to facts we may have overlooked. A good prayer is, "Almighty God, our Heavenly Creator, unto whom all hearts are open, all desires known, and from whom no secrets are hid, cleanse the thoughts of our hearts by the inspiration of thy Holy Spirit, that we may perfectly love thee, and worthily magnify thy holy name, through Jesus Christ our Lord. Amen."

Through the centuries men and women have found the Bible a lamp unto our feet. Read quickly and then go back and read slowly. Write down any message you feel you have received and then test it. A professor at Union Theological Seminary tells of two Christian women visiting a family friend in prison. He was unresponsive, so they left a Bible. Only after the man's execution did they find a note in which he told how he began reading about Jesus before Pilate, his prayer for his enemies, and then this man said, "I felt a stab at my heart. I don't know what I felt, but I know I did believe." The Bible is quicker than a two-edged sword. It is a revealer of truth.

The Holy Spirit guides through the inner voice. We sometimes dull this conscience. Every year the Federal Government receives anonymously from many people a rather large sum of money which they call "conscience money." We may smother this inner voice for years, but usually, sooner or later, it breaks through to haunt us. The inner voice has not only the negative value of checking us when we are inclined toward evil, but it also can be an inner guide toward truth and victory. The Bible says "spirit with spirit can meet." God's Spirit and our human spirit can have joyous concourse.

CHAPTER SIX

BIBLE

 ince there is no creed to which all United Methodists must yield allegiance, then by what methods·can our doctrinal reflection and construction be most fruitful and fulfilling? This question is raised by the Doctrinal Statement. The answer comes in terms of our free inquiry within the boundaries defined by four main sources and guidelines for Christian theology: scripture, tradition, experience, and reason. They provide a broad and stable context for reflection and formulation. They instruct us as we carry forward our never-ending tasks of theologizing.

Primary Source

If scripture is one of the guidelines for theologizing, for working out our beliefs, what are some of the understandings we bring to the Bible as United Methodists? We believe that while it is only one of the guidelines, it is nevertheless the primary source for doctrine. We never forget that Christian doctrine has been formed, consciously and unconsciously, from metaphors and themes, the origins of which are biblical. "The Bible is the deposit of a unique testimony to God's self-disclosures: in the world's creation, redemption and final fulfillment; in Jesus Christ as the incarnation of God's Word; in the Holy Spirit's constant activity in the dramas of history. It is the primitive source of the memories, images and hopes by which the Christian community came into existence and that still confirm and nourish its faith and understanding." This statement, coming from the work of the Theological Commission, reveals much of our official stance on the matter of scripture. We are not literalists; we do not hold to the old notion that it is without error in matters of history and scientific suggestion. We do believe that as we open our minds and hearts to the Word of God through the words of persons inspired by the Holy Spirit, faith is born and nourished, and "both the core of faith and the range of our theological opinions are expanded and enriched."

We do not believe in the method of "proof-texting," that is, finding a passage and then lifting it out of its context in support of some particular idea. We do affirm scripture texts "are rightly interpreted in the light of their place in the Bible as a whole, and this is illumined by scholarly inquiry and personal insight." It is obvious that the meaning of each text is best understood when its original intention and significance have been grasped. We also believe that there is a practical relevance to the study of scripture. When it is carefully handled, under the guidance of the Holy Spirit, "we may apply the truth to the circumstances of our time and place."

With these ideas from our Doctrinal Statement in the *Book of Discipline* as background, let us now examine in some detail what this means for us. First, the Bible is the source of the "memories, images, and hopes by which the Christian community came into existence." All this was dramatized and brought to focus when the Assembly of the World Council of Churches developed and enlarged the definition of the World Council. The definition originally was this: "It is a fellowship of churches which accept our Lord Jesus Christ as God and Saviour." Succinct and simple—there it was. Now two things happened to bring about an enlargement of the definition. The first was the inclusion of the Russian Orthodox Church which brought a conviction that there should be a reference to the Holy Trinity. The second was a feeling on the part of many Protestant churches that there should be some reference made to scripture. Combining these two emphases, the definition was enlarged to read: "The World Council of Churches is a fellowship of churches which confess the Lord Jesus Christ as God and Saviour according to the Holy Scripture, and therefore seek to fulfill their common calling to the glory of one God, Father, Son, and Holy Spirit." Through this proclamation of the new definition, we have brought into focus the relevance of the scriptures for the Christian tradition.

A second thought relates to inspiration. Some rigid theories of verbal inspiration of the Bible hold that the human author was simply a mouthpiece of God; God dictated the Bible, so that every word represents the divine mind. A mechanical theory of inspiration is rejected by most United Methodist scholars who view the scriptures as historically conditioned, although they do believe the Holy Spirit was acting upon the human agent. One way of suggesting this idea is the approach taken by Luther. He said that God is in every syllable, but Luther still recognized errors and inconsistencies in the scriptures. For example, he saw the differences between the birth stories in Matthew and Luke. He also recognized that some books were of more value than others. He said the Epistle of James is an epistle of straw. In other words, the principle of inspiration was accepted, uniformity of inspiration was not. Inspiration does not mean verbal dictation. Most scholars conclude that it is the truths which are inspired and not the words, which are merely the vehicles of truth. It is important to distinguish between word-pictures and the truth they are intended to convey.

How should we, with all our knowledge of physics, biology, and geology, of anthropology, paleontology, and astronomy, understand such biblical stories as the creation of humankind, the stories of devils and demons, of speaking animals? Are not these stories a flagrant contradiction of what modern science and technology tell us?

Rudolph Bultmann, who stirred considerable controversy with his essay "The New Testament and Mythology," stressed that we are to take these stories seriously. But they require interpretation. He calls this process demythologizing. The biblical message has come to us in the language and thought patterns of the people whom God moved to write it.

That ancient world view, Bultmann says, is "mythological" over against the rational-scientific worldview of our time with its different emphasis on cause-and-effect relationships. We must, therefore, interpret the biblical message in the categories in which modern men and women tend to think. Further, rather than reject myth as a lie, we can read some biblical stories with great benefit because they teach us true things about our world and faith.

There are over eleven hundred known human languages. A translator must use extreme ingenuity to convey sense and truth where word-for-word transmission is out of the question. You cannot talk to tribes who live without ever seeing navigable water of our possessing "an anchor of the soul." You cannot speak to the Eskimos of "the lamb of God" or of Christ being "the true vine."

Paul was struggling with human words to express something of the wonders which, he sensed, lay beyond observable life. When he spoke of Christ ascending "up on high" he was not really talking of some location a certain number of miles above the earth's surface. We talk of high ideals or of a high purpose or of a failing business as going downhill. In similar fashion Paul used expressions of height and depth as useful symbols but not as geographical locations. The New Testament uses picture language. But we do that. The accountant speaks of frozen assets, and the town-planner refers to a "bottle-neck." There is, however, a real situation behind each of the short-hand pictures and there is a reality behind every Christian expression. Because picture language is sometimes used, it does not follow that the actual events are unhistorical or false.

At one time the Roman Catholic catechism had this question: "Who founded the Roman Catholic church?" and the answer given was, "Jesus Christ." The next question read, "Who founded other denominations and churches?" and the answer was, "Ordinary people like you and me." In this ecumenical age this set of questions is rarely used. But the appropriate answer could be "both."

How We Got Our Bible

We believe the Bible is a result of the efforts of both the Holy Spirit and ordinary persons. Furthermore, all churches were founded by ordinary persons even as they strove to embody the teaching and the spirit of Jesus Christ. The work of ordinary men and women can be seen as we trace their contribution in bringing the Bible down the ages to us.

Not one single word of the original writings remains. The ancient Hebrew people had sacred writings. We do have copies of various biblical books and other fragments dating back to 150 B.C. and found near the Dead Sea. These writings were referred to as "The Law," "The Prophets," "Other Sacred Writings." All were written in ancient Hebrew characters.

In about 200 B.C. a group of "learned fathers," seventy in all, gathered in Alexandria, Egypt and carefully collected and translated their Sacred Writings into Greek, primarily for the use of the Jews in that area. But the Jews in Egypt and the Jews in Palestine could not agree upon what constituted the "Holy Writings" since there were many other similar writings claiming authenticity. The Alexandrians wished to include many of the Apocryphal Books, while the Palestinian Jews stood for the list of Books as we have them in our Authorized Version. The latter, the Old Testament as we have it, without the Apocrypha which is in the Catholic Bible, constitutes the scriptures which Jesus knew and from which he quoted.

During the latter part of the first century A.D. the New Testament books were completed. They came from many sources, and there is no common theme through them all. They were written in Aramaic and Greek. They were widely distributed, read, passed to others. Athanasius, bishop of Alexandria, promulgated a canonical New Testament list in his Easter letter of A.D. 367. This list is famous as the first to include all the books found in our New Testament today.

The first great translation of the Bible into a living language was the "Vulgate" in Latin, completed by Jerome in Bethlehem, about A.D. 400. Revised and retranslated by a Church Council it remains as the Douay Version which has been the official Bible of the Roman Catholic Church.

Wycliffe completed the first translation of the Bible into English or Saxon in 1382. It was handwritten and so highly prized that there is the record of one eager Christian who gave a load of hay in order that he might have a day with a copy of the scripture. Tyndale finished the first real translation into the common language of the people. This was published in 1525 and was one of the first books printed. He was martyred for his effort because there was considerable opposition to putting the scripture in the language of the people. Church authorities feared that if it were available to the people they would misinterpret its meaning and corrupt its influence. Then in 1611 there was the Authorized Version which we familiarly call the King James Version. This was a scholarly and consecrated attempt to revise, correct, and harmonize all previous translations. The beauty, grandeur, and magnificence of this translation have never been surpassed, though in sales it is falling behind newer versions.

The influence of scripture on Western civilization cannot be overemphasized. Our conversation is liberally sprinkled with phrases out of the scripture. We speak of "the salt of the earth," "apple of the eye," "skin of the teeth," "filthy lucre," "labor of love," and "beating our spears into plowshares." All these phrases are lifted directly out of the scripture.

It was the judgment of H. G. Wells that "the Bible has been the Book that held together the fabric of western civilization. It has been the handbook of life to countless millions of men and women. The civilization we possess could not have come into existence and could not have been sustained without it."

We are simply trying to say that the Bible is a very human book in its origins and translations, and has profoundly influenced our human institutions in Western civilization. But it also contains the inspired Word of God. Carried with the ancient figures of speech which it uses to express its ideas, the careful and serious reader finds within the Bible eternal truths which will serve to guide him or her in the search for the meaning of life. It will be necessary to improve our mechanical equipment and redesign our scientific instruments, but we will never find it necessary to amend the great moral and spiritual principles which it sets forth.

For years J. B. Phillips, a noted scholar in Great Britain, looked upon the scriptures with something akin to disdain. He was a linguist, and after spending years with classical Greek he considered New Testament Greek in about the same category as a Shakespearean scholar would consider the weekly letter from the pastor to the congregation. During World War II he remembered Paul's letters were written to those in danger. "As I began translating these epistles," he later wrote, "my conviction grew that the New Testament was in a quite special sense inspired. It is not magical; nor is it faultless. Human beings wrote it. But by something which I would not hesitate to describe as a miracle there is a concentration upon that area of inner truth which is fundamental and ageless. That, I believe, is the reason why millions of people have heard the voice of God speaking to them through these seemingly artless pages."

Authority

Medieval thinking was dominated by the idea of authority. This idea was generally derived from the tradition of the elders and the dicta of the church as the depository, guardian, and interpreter of that tradition. The historic continuity of the faith was the major emphasis when talking about authority. Thinking was rigidly controlled, and nothing that we now know as freedom and scholarship was tolerated or even conceivable. The argument that tradition was more important than scripture rested on the assertion that the church existed before the Bible. Authority for the Roman Catholic derived from the church, which was headed by the living representative of Christ, the Pope. The church was the depository of "the truth delivered by our elders," and private judgment in the interpretation of scriptures was denied.

The Reformation was a break with this attitude. The Reformers maintained that the authority for the doctrines which they held rested on scripture. In other words, the basis for authority in the Reformation church was shifted from the church headed by the Pope to the "Scriptural precedent and primitive example." This point of view generally still prevails in Protestantism and is illustrated by the fact that when new members are received into The United Methodist Church the question is asked: "Do you receive and profess the Christian faith as contained in the scriptures of the Old and New Testaments?" The faith found in the scripture is what binds us. There is no hierarchial structure within United Methodism that has authority over the individual in spiritual matters. The General Conference may speak for us in issues that pertain to polity and structure, but in the matters of the faith it can only speak to us of emphases and offer guidelines. The source of authority for the individual is in scripture.

This is an age, however, that raises questions, not only about the authority of the Bible but about the value of all authority. What is the point of teaching or studying the classical disciplines, including the Bible, when the bases for our action are given with sufficient clarity by contemporary ethics and the adjunct studies of sociology and psychology? I suspect many of us, if our back were against the wall, would honestly have to answer, "Very little indeed." There is probably a widespread, intuitive acceptance of two affirmations: (1) The New Testament and the creeds are no longer in any way authoritative or canonical for us; (2) Christians today can find sufficient guidelines for their faith and action in contemporary statements and solutions.

Without disrespect, we can admit that the Bible does not have scientific authority in the material realm. Christianity was originally propagated in an age ignorant of the scientific facts that began to come to light with the Copernican revolution in cosmology. But let's not worry too much about that. Even the astronauts made reference to "sunset," and of all people they knew that was not a scientific truth, but they did not let technical knowledge rob them of the spiritual insights that are a valid witness to truth.

Remember this: The Bible does have the authority of valid human experience. Experience is costly and sometimes painful. Unfortunately, as a proverb reminds us, experience is like giving an expensive comb to a man who has lost his hair. You have learned from the experience, but now it's too late. Reading the scripture is a way of learning from the experiences of others. We do not observe the Ten Commandments simply because they are in the scripture. If this were the only reason for observing them, most of us would not heed their counsel. We feel that the Ten Commandments are true because they are the summation, they are the crystallization of the experiences of earlier generations. They say to us, "If you want to know how to live creatively, meaningfully, then here are guides that will help you."

It also has the authority of spiritual truth. Consider its insights. You feel you have done your best. What next? Paul tells the Ephesians in four words: "Having done all . . . stand" (6:13). Relax, stand quietly, quit trying to overcome with just your conscious mind. "Underneath are the everlasting arms." One of the deepest forms of communication is touch. We are born with the fear of falling. The idea of being sustained with loving arms speaks to our need for security. "Love thy neighbor as thyself." Lack of self-esteem is the most common emotional ailment. Read the story of the Prodigal Son. How can we feel permanently rejected or condemned with this magnificent promise: "Take no thought for the morrow!" A modern rephrasing might be, "Stop worrying about the future." "Sufficient unto the day are the evils thereof." We have problems right now. "They that wait upon the Lord shall mount up with wings of eagles." "Where your treasure is, there will your heart be also." We know the validity of this. What is important to you? "You will know the truth and the truth will make you free!" The goal of psychotherapy is to bring us to that place where we have the strength to face the truth about ourselves. Spiritual truth is more than cognitive; it is relational, personal, inner, and life-changing. "What is man . . . you have crowned him a little lower than the angels." On this affirmation about the dignity of persons rests our concept of freedom and democracy. Western civilization has drawn upon the biblical idea of humankind for its definition of government.

Read Your Bible

The Bible does carry the authority of valid spiritual insights—truths tested by the centuries of human experience. We are not, however, a Bible reading people. In a certain high school English class, 88 percent of the students could not name the four Gospels. One student said that three of them are Christianity, Hinduism, and confusion, but he didn't know the fourth. At the University of Denver, a student was asked on a test, "Tell what you know about Moses." He answered frankly, "All I know about Moses is that he is dead."

Our neglect of the Bible, while unfortunate, is understandable. The occasional Bible reader is overwhelmed by the strangeness of the Bible's content. It is a conglomeration of material on a wide variety of subjects, written on two continents, in three languages, by many different authors scattered over a thousand years. Furthermore, there are so many difficult questions. The Gospel of Luke tells us that Jesus was born of a virgin. Yet the Gospel of Matthew traces his genealogy back to David through Joseph. How do you reconcile that? Why do we have four gospels instead of one, when they tell the same basic story? Why two Old Testament histories—Kings and Chronicles? Who can understand all the imagery of Revelation? How did the erotic passages in Ezekiel and the Song of Solomon ever slip by the censors?

All this, however, should not deter us in our effort to understand and apply the scripture. The simple fact is that this literary expression of the religious development of the Hebrew people culminating in the life and teachings of Jesus is required reading for those who would call themselves Christian. The Bible is the story of Jesus Christ. He is the unifying principle. He gives meaning to the Old Testament. Our doctrinal statement would remind us that "the Bible is the deposit of a unique testimony to God's self-disclosures . . . in Jesus Christ as the incarnation of God's Word." The procession of laws, genealogies and love songs, of ancient history, priests and prophets, of faith and despair, make sense because it all leads to Christ. This is, for the Christian, the basic reason for studying the Bible. William Warren Smart once said, "There is probably not a person living who could, over a considerable period of time, spend twenty minutes a day in the presence of Jesus as the Gospels have pictured him without having his life profoundly influenced by him one way or another."

When we look at Christ we remember that God is identified with our condition. Elie Wiesel, a gifted Israeli journalist, spent years in a concentration camp and was overwhelmed by the evidence of evil in his fellow prisoners and in his surroundings. One day he was forced to watch the hanging of a young boy by the Gestapo, a hanging that lasted more than half an hour because the boy's body was so light. As he strangled to death in indescribable agony, most of his fellow prisoners stood in stunned silence. One man spoke for them all as he cried out repeatedly, "Where is God now? Where is God now?" Deep within his own life, Elie Wiesel was certain of the answer, "God is there on the gallows—dead."

But George McLeod affirmed it this way: "Jesus Christ was not crucified in a cathedral between two candles, but on a cross between two thieves; on the town garbage heap; on a crossroads so cosmopolitan that they had to write his title in Hebrew and Latin and Greek; at the kind of place where cynics talk smut, and thieves curse, and soldiers gamble. Because this is where he died, and that is what he died about."

The Bible makes it plain that God is not dead but involved in all that hurts and destroys the vision and hope of humankind. The men and women of the Bible were making an honest search for God. They struggled with doubt and fear and uncertainty. As the Bible talks about this, no questions are avoided; no issues evaded; no difficulties glossed over. And through it all looms the figure of one who was crucified between two thieves at the crossroads, revealing a God who touches us in the moment of need and struggle.

When we look to the Christ revealed in scripture, we discover God's call to mission. We know of God's mandate. As we look at Christ, we know what God is like and what is expected of us. And the call is to "take up your cross and come follow me."

When we look to the Christ revealed in scripture, we catch a vision of the hope eternal! At a recent discussion about the church, a young person said, "I don't want to hear any more sermons about heaven! Heaven can wait! I want help now on how to live each day as I face choices about drugs, sex, career, and marriage. I could care less about heaven!" This is an understandable feeling. When we are young the issues of the moment are so urgent. It is our faith that Jesus, who died relatively young, could understand this. In fact, a "rich young ruler" came running to him with a request for additional knowledge about the secrets of life. But there comes a moment when the decisions of drugs, sex, and career are no longer paramount. We yearn for something "beyond." We are ready to go home.

Bible reading can be more meaningful if one of the modern translations is used. The King James version was an effort to put the scripture into the language of its day. The Bible is more understandable if it is read in the idiom of our day. Second, buy a commentary. This will give the background of each book, the author, to whom the book was written, for what purpose and outline, and the central idea or theme. With this in mind, the message becomes more easily discernible. Third, keep your Bible available. Many carry a small vest-pocket edition of the New Testament to use when there are a few spare moments available. Daily reading can give a new sense of direction and balance.

It is important to be selective in reading. Don't start with Genesis and read toward Revelation. It is a library, not a book. Start with the Gospel of Mark, for with its sharp reportorial style one can get an insight into the Man of Galilee. Move from that into the story of Acts where the heroism of those who established the missionary church is recorded. Reach into the Old Testament and study some of the ancestors of the faith. Listen to the music in the style of the Apostle Paul, particularly in First Corinthians. When in a reflective mood try some of the Psalms. If we read selectively, knowing a little of the background, the message will come alive and speak to our deepest need.

Above all, read it devotionally. Let the Holy Spirit speak through the sacred pages. It is not healthy to be overly concerned about passages that seem difficult or contain apparent contradictions. Always approach it with the question, "What is God saying to me from these pages of Holy Writ?" Read it to catch the mind and spirit of the heroes of the faith. Read it to discover Christ. And when you do this, you will find a fire and zeal kindling in your own heart that will bring you to the portals of heaven!

CHAPTER SEVEN

CHURCH

 "The United Methodist view of faith and its fruits is linked with a distinctive emphasis on polity. In our understanding of the church, there has been a long-standing tension between our original image of small, voluntary 'religious societies' organized for Christian fellowship, and the worldwide church which has developed in the course of two centuries. . . . On the one hand, the basic premise of the small group is the principle of 'subsidiarity' or voluntary association and local initiative. It is in the local communities and in small groups within them that the Holy Spirit nurtures meaningful experiences which then seek wider avenues of mission and outreach. On the other hand, United Methodists, believing themselves led by the same Spirit, have a long tradition of connectional administration which binds us together in seeing our task as a whole, in efficient planning, and in deploying our material and human resources."

This statement implies a need for the organized community of believers and suggests the church has two responsibilities. The first is to provide the setting in which the Holy Spirit can nurture meaningful religious experience. The second is to "connect" with other congregations in such a way that there can be effective deploying of material and human resources.

Let us first examine the question as to the necessity of any organization. A youth delegate to an annual conference said, "We have Jesus; why do we need the church?" We are committed to the idea that even in the midst of a revolutionary time in church history, one that may alter radically the present structuring of congregational life, the established community of believers is still an instrument through which the Holy Spirit may work and few of us are willing to rush out and commit institutional suicide.

When Karl Barth made his lecture tour here in the States not too long before his death, he said: "When theology confronts the Word of God and its witnesses, its place is very concretely in the community, not somewhere in empty space. . . . It is the commonwealth gathered, founded, and ordered by the Word of God, the 'Communion of Saints.' " T. S. Eliot once asked a pertinent question, "What life have you if you have not life together? There is no life that is not in community, and no community not lived in praise of God."

Why We Need the Church

There is still the need for the quietly committed institutional church where people worship, respond to preaching, study in classes, and share in fellowship. A pastor on Chicago's South Side, while doing research for Methodism's Bicentennial, came across an intriguing idea. "George Whitefield," he said, "was a greater preacher than Francis Asbury but little came from Whitefield's oratory because it was never organized. Asbury was not so eloquent but he left us the Methodist Church." Then he continued, "Side by side in Chicago slums I witnessed secularly-oriented churches become conformed to the world. Community renewal, let alone Christian renewal, did not stem from these. It was the worshipping congregation in that slum area that showed a real sense of spiritual power and which, in the long pull, demonstrated the resources for both personal and community renewal. It was a quietly committed institutional church which was the real guts of hope in a seemingly hopeless situation. Where God was placed above man and love of man was an imperative stemming from love and worship of God, the institution renewed itself and became a growing force in the renewal of the community." It is our conviction as United Methodists that when all the innovations have been tried and all the theories promoted, there will still be a need for the people of God to join together in worship, thus equipping themselves for their ministries.

Harvey Cox has reminded us that our generation may be more religious in expression, but less religious in institution. It is true that institutions may become introverted, self-serving, lacking in abrasive, and insensitive to their original missionary impulse. Nevertheless, we still say a word in behalf of some kind of organization for, when the Spirit is present, there is a thrust toward servanthood and community, and this must be coordinated.

Acts 4:32 is a forerunner of the modern commune, for it says that "the company of those who believed were of one heart and soul, and . . . had everything in common." This would require organized cooperation. Chapter six indicates that there was a division of responsibility in the early church as they picked seven men, full of the Spirit, to serve tables. In First Corinthians the Apostle Paul points out that there are varieties of gifts and varieties of service but the same Spirit. And he makes it quite clear that, when the Spirit comes, there is unity in diversity; there is harmony; and there is organization for the purposes of the divine mission.

The "Religion in America Series" has a book by Charles Ferguson on the Methodists and the making of America. It is titled *Organizing to Beat the Devil.* The author reminds us that the Greeks had a word for it, but the United Methodists have a pamphlet for it. He concludes by saying that our omnipresent sense of legal order and parliamentary procedure can be summed up in the apocryphal story of the action of the official board of laypersons in a local church who, upon hearing that their pastor was ill, voted thirteen to twelve to pray for him.

Mr. Ferguson tells of Charles McCabe, an Ohio preacher who, in 1862, enlisted in the war against the Confederacy. He was captured and put in a prison for officers in Richmond. Since he possessed the Methodist penchant for organization, he immediately divided his fellow prisoners into classes and by using the various talents in the group, he established the "University of Libby Prison." He is best remembered, however, as a singer who popularized the "Battle Hymn of the Republic." His many talents were acknowledged and rewarded by the church which elected him a Bishop.

On one occasion, he was asked to preside at the General Conference. Soon, there were about a dozen motions on the floor and the parliamentary procedure had degenerated into an uproar. He pounded the gavel and said: "The brethren are getting restless. Let's stand and sing." He broke into the opening lines of "In the Sweet Bye and Bye." The clamor subsided as the delegates began: "There's a land that is fairer than day, and by faith we can see it afar." After the hymn, according to legend, Bishop McCabe said: "By faith we can see the promised land; but we had better get organized if we are going to get there!"

The Spirit brings liberation, but the faith must be nurtured by a community of believers. High resolves need the reinforcement of the group. When people start looking in the same direction, they are drawn together, and this results in some kind of organization.

We have been saying that organization and "connectionalism" are necessary if we are to have much effectiveness. There must be the instrument by which human and material resources can be deployed. There is also, however, a need for recognizing the concept of "subsidiarity," that is, maintaining the small group concept where the spiritual nature can be nurtured and where men and women can meet God. This is basically why the church exists.

Paul made reference to the prophetic charisma. Peter defended the apostles on the day of Pentecost by saying that they were not drunk but that God had poured out his Spirit upon them and sons and daughters were prophesying.

The Contemporary Church

Louis Armstrong once said about jazz music: "If I have to explain it to you, then you ain't got it." Perhaps we can't explain all that this suggests, but I think it means that the contemporary church must not be afraid of the emotional, the mystical, the subjective, the devotional. For it is this that humanizes life.

A church is not some kind of machine to produce money for headquarters or grind out figures for a statistical column. It is people who dream dreams; who have visions; who get drunk out of frustration; who sweat so their kids can have a chance; who one day love, the next day fight with their marriage partners; who sometimes come to church when they would rather play golf; and who finally die of a coronary or carcinoma. Through it all they are so hungry for a real taste of God that it is often like a sharp pain down deep! Frankly, you should not go to any church unless it offers you an outside chance of a glimpse of God that literally takes away your breath and knocks you to your knees.

In an issue of the "Kiplinger Washington Letter," there was this word of instruction for retailers: "Pay more attention to changing fads, styles . . . notice what the youngsters are doing and wearing, what interests them, what TV shows they tune in. Why? To keep your stocks 'hot'. . . . Customers are young and getting younger. But many retailers are middle-aged . . . and may disapprove of young-sters' styles. Bad mistake." The church must be responsive to the requirements of the one-half of the American population that is under twenty-seven. We must remember their experiences.

Martin Marty, church historian and associate editor of *The Christian Century*, has indicated that the spread of the occult and of Eastern religions is giving Christianity a needed nudge toward its original moorings. He has said: "We have been so busy in Christianity in recent years that we've stopped meditating. Now the fashionable Eastern religions are teaching the younger generation to be still and to know that God is God and to meditate. I do not think that Buddhism is going to replace Christianity, nor that astrology is going to replace Judaism. Rather, there will be a kind of rebirth of a sense of wonder and mystery which are dimensions of our faith we have let drop."

In an effort to respond to this movement, many churches are trying to take a second look at the experiential and emotional developments without falling prey to the excesses of the "grope-and-touch" groups or "body-celebration" traps. They are trying to understand the revival of transcendental impulses and the survival of Pentecostal forms in some of the traditional churches even when put off by some of the less lovable aspects.

What all this means is the suggestion that we seek a church that is not afraid of the dimension of subjective experience. Find a church that understands that it exists for one fundamental reason: to help create conditions in which you may encounter God. Don't worry about the old arguments about pietism versus activism. This is about as silly as arguing about which is more important, to inhale or exhale. Any religion worthy of the name will include both.

The recent years have brought many changes to the church. During the 1950s there was the exhilaration of popular acceptance—banners flying—and of numerical growth. In the 1960s, there was often a sense of ambiguity, of uncertainty, even of embarrassment. Our theological notes were muted and our role lacked precise definition. We felt left out of things by intoxicating but remotely based movements. Now that radical theology has virtually passed and revolutionary calls are some-what silenced, with youth on university campuses more conservative, we, on the local scene, overwhelmed by a sense of realism about the limits of human possibility, nevertheless feel it has fallen to the parish situation to make some small dent on a world of injustice.

A sociologist was recently asked why men and women enroll in divinity schools. His answer may not speak for you, but this is the way he viewed it. He said:

> Almost nobody goes to win a good name or honor. They enroll because many of them awaken during college to the fact that religion is one of the few approaches to humanizing the world. . . . They despair of other societal institutions and have some hope that religion and its institutions—weak, frail, and self-serving as they may be—are more malleable to change and provide an opportunity to serve.

There was a fellow who caught a taxi during a torrential rain. He complained to the driver: "This weather is terrible." To this the driver responded: "It's better than none."

We hold up the local church as a possible arena for service if for no other reason than the one: "It's better than none!" The fact remains that the local church can provide a handle for doing something about our neglected elderly in America. It may not be reaching them, but it is an institution that has access to some three-fourths of our youth. It has a chance to minister to blue-collar, ethnic America. It is right in the middle of the boredom and drama of suburbia.

The church is not only the community of service, but also of love. Jesus, "The Man for Others," sought the support of the twelve, precarious as their companionship proved to be. For millions of persons, loneliness is an ever-present, dull pain. One of the things the church has rediscovered in recent years is that fellowship is intrinsic to the faith rather than being something that is added. Koinonia groups for prayer, witness, and study are again flourishing. The concept of the "Body of Christ," with the members responsible for one another, is once more a living reality.

Recently, a Yokefellow group wrote a paraphrase of Matthew 11:28-30. It reads:

> When you feel weighed down by physical, mental, or spiritual burdens, open your heart to my love, because I want very much to help you. Put your hand in mine and let's walk the road of life

together. Listen to what I say to you, because what I say will be to help you, not to hurt you. I love you and understand you deeply. I don't expect you to be self-sufficient or equal to every situation, but I am ready to be with you and help you every minute of every day. . . . I only ask you to take the share of the weight you are ready and eager to carry.

If somewhere, somehow, you can discover this kind of vital, Spirit-filled community, rejoice, for indeed, your reward is great. Cherish it as a gift of God. To discover this kind of mutual trust is to taste for yourself the fruit of the Spirit.

The Future of Our Church

There has been a lot of negative thinking. Notice the headlines. "United Methodist Church loses members." "Church attendance continues to sag!" What do these headlines mean for those of us who have responsibility within the local church?

It has been quite popular in recent years to refer to this as a "post-Christian world." Bonhoeffer coined an interesting phrase, "religionless Christianity." That is, the faith might survive but you would not see any outward expression of it. John Cardinal Wright, when serving as an American advisor at the Vatican, said: "This is the winter for Christianity. It will continue until something cataclysmic happens."

Let's look at the positive attitude. First, God will not be without a witness. We may or may not be a part of it, but the witness will be there. Hitler said the church was hollow and he could destroy it in a year, but the church has been an anvil on which a good many hammers have worn out.

Second, the large picture may not be as gloomy as some people predict. A newspaper had an article about church attendance and quoted the Gallup Poll. The headline read, "Catholic *churchgoing* down: Protestant rate is constant." The percentage in Protestantism has changed little in recent years; the Catholics have declined 10 to 20 percent. Giving is at an all-time high.

Third, this is not a post-Christian world. Someone, writing about this, says that this would suggest there was a time when the world was Christian. When did this exist? Was it in the days of the early church, the days of pagan Rome, the era of the martyrs? Was it the fourth century when Constantine proclaimed Christianity the official religion of the empire and then used it primarily as a tool of conquest, massacre, and slavery?

Was it the Dark Ages, the very adjective description denying the principle that Christ is the light of the world? Could it have been the Middle Ages, when life was crude, boorish, and short?

Would you apply the term *Christian* to the eighteenth and nineteenth centuries, the age of slavery, colonialism, industrial exploitation? And certainly it was not the first half of the twentieth century when the chief condition was war upon war, each one stooping more deeply into savagery and barbarity. So when did the Christian era ever exist?

There is as much opportunity in our age as any. In fact, we may be on the verge of some startling developments. Stephen Neill, in *Call to Mission* predicts that Africa by the year 2000 will be the most Christian of the continents. One reason for this is that 80 percent of the literate people in tropical Africa received at least a part of their education in the mission schools. With the demise of the old tribal religions, there is a vacuum into which the Christian faith can move, and the African people are acquainted with its truth.

Fourth, it is well to remember, when the going is difficult, that Christianity was never a majority force. Christians always seem to be a little on the wrong side of history, or a little out of step. But this is precisely the point. It is through a dedicated minority that God's work gets done. The notion of a saving remnant is still valid. Jesus spoke of his disciples as the leaven working in the loaf, as salt giving flavor to the whole. Louis Cassels made reference to the fact that the Christian church, in every generation, is saved by a cadre of dedicated men and women who take the cross. It's never a mass movement! The Reverend R. W. Hugh Jones delivered a presidential address to the annual Assembly of the Congregational Church in England and Wales. Speaking in Westminster Chapel, he said; "We are frightened by falling numbers. Sometimes we are urgently concerned with numbers because we are absorbed by and obsessed with the thought of making the church successful. The very thought is irrelevant. We are not here to make the church successful. We are here to burn ourselves out in service for Christ. This is the only valid interpretation of success. But this is not always the image we project. More frequently it is that of men sitting around a table, grey with anxiety wondering how to raise enough money to preach the gospel which tells men not to be anxious."

Fifth, there is a hunger, an openness, a searching for spiritual truth. It is in, for example, the large number of message songs, produced by the media. *The New York Times,* reviewing records, said: "If there is any news in the pop record world today, it is that the influence of the gospel—which Webster defines as the good news concerning Christ—is preempting the influence of almost everything else."

When our Lord said we must become like children, we take it to mean trust, receptivity, and simplicity; but what typifies the child more is curiosity. With this in mind, the religious outlook is by no means as gloomy as some would have us believe. If we refuse to be sandbagged by statistics of church membership and influence and instead listen to the living voice of this generation, we can't miss the note of awakening religious curiosity. College students may stay away from chapel in droves, but they are demanding courses in religion as never before. You can find Kierkegaard, Tillich, Kahlil Gibran, Augustine, and the Koran jostling among the textbooks and the pornography on any bookrack.

The contemporary church must regain a sense of victory and purpose, however, if it is to meet the expressed hunger for spiritual reality. Sociologist Peter Berger gave an address at the annual meeting of the Consultation on Church Union. He bluntly told the ecumenists that their efforts to regroup as one big church were a waste of time unless Protestantism regained its self-confidence. He said, "It is time to stop asking what modern man has to say to the church and to turn to the more significant question, 'What does the church have to say to modern man?' " Then Mr. Berger answered his own question. He said: "It's the old story of God's dealings with man spanning the Exodus to Easter morn." The church is custodian of the message for which the world hungers.

CHAPTER EIGHT

CONVERSION

ur Doctrinal Statement affirms that "another United Methodist family trait has been an active stress on conversion and a new birth. Whatever our language or labels for it, we hold that a decisive change in the human heart can and does occur under the promptings of grace and the guidance of the Holy Spirit. Such a change may be sudden, dramatic, gradual, cumulative. Always it is a new beginning in a process. Christian experience as personal transformation expresses itself in many different thought-forms and lifestyles. All of these have a common feature: faith working by love."

Born Again

No theme has been more central to United Methodists than the necessity of the "New Birth." Our passion for evangelism grows out of the firm conviction that we must be "born again." We believe there is no substitute for this. John's Gospel reports that early in the ministry of Jesus a Jewish ruler, Nicodemus, visited him to inquire the way to the kingdom of God. Even though he had wealth, status, and a noble heritage, Nicodemus had a spiritual hunger that moved him to seek Jesus. An astute man, he began the conversation by complimenting Jesus, saying that no one could do what he was doing unless God was with him. Jesus responded to this with the abrupt affirmation: "You must be born anew" (John 3:7).

Few passages of scripture have been more variously interpreted than this imperative: "Be born again," or, "Be born anew." To many it is as bewildering a concept as it was to Nicodemus. The unchurched think of it as vaguely related to revivalist preaching and exhortation. They shrug it aside because they want no part of what they consider to be some kind of emotionalism. Because of such unfortunate association, the person on the street and even many within the church have been inclined to disregard the whole concept of conversion as unnecessary or even undesirable.

The best of our theologians, however, have not so regarded it. Edwin Lewis, for many years a distinguished professor of theology at Drew University, wrote: "Jesus confronted the astonished Nicodemus . . . (and) told him that the purpose of a man's being born once was that he might be born a second time, and until he was born a second time the purpose of his being born the first time remained unfulfilled." " 'That which is born of the flesh is flesh.' This is creaturehood. 'That which is born of the Spirit is spirit.' This is sonship."

God's purpose for us has not been fulfilled until we have been born of the Spirit! This assertion moves the new birth out of the area of life's options to the place of focal concern. Method and mode are not particularly important, but each person stands in need of a radical and fundamental reorientation of life at the very center. There must be a confrontation with his or her need of reconciliation to God. There must be a transformation.

This change will have both subjective and objective implications. This is more than an intellectual assent to a system of principles. The will must come into play. There must be a faith-response of repentance (new direction) and a receiving by faith of grace (acceptance of God's unmerited love and forgiveness). With this act of saving faith, life assumes a new direction.

When we begin a discussion of the "New Birth," however, the skeptic is entitled to wonder if human nature can be changed. We know change is in the natural order. When friends whom you have not seen for many months come to visit, your first comment to the children is usually, "My, how you've changed." But not only do children grow. All around us is process and change. Nothing in creation is fixed and static. Birth, growth, death, and rebirth is the cycle in the natural order.

Human Nature

But what of that thing we call human nature? Webster defines it as the essential qualities or peculiar attributes which constitute humankind. Can this be changed? A young man confessed that he was in the grip of a vicious habit. Then he added, "I've given up all hope of ever being able to change." But even as he made the assertion, you had the feeling that he wanted to be assured that he could gain a victory. The Bible and church tradition have much to say about this matter. 'We shall examine four of the ideas. The *first* is found in Genesis 1:26 where we read: "Then God said, 'Let us make (humankind) in our image, after our likeness.'" Christian tradition has always affirmed that there is a divine spirit within us which we call "the image of God." One theologian has written, "It is not possible for my faith to be shaken by man, however low he may sink; for this faith is not grounded on what man thinks about man, but on what God thinks about him. . . . There has not been enough emphasis on man: there has not been emphasis on man to the point of affirming him in God." This is a vital distinction. We may write off each other as animalistic and of little significance but God says, "Let us make (humankind) in our image."

Scientists quite properly devote much effort to analyzing humankind. We are physically measured, socially evaluated, and mentally tested. But our spirit, which "the image of God" suggests, cannot be contained or schematized. The life and spirit of men and women are not substantial realities which can be held in the hand and docketed and described. They can only be expressed, and when expressed in relationship to the Creator, they give us a glory and a distinctiveness.

We are born again only when we say yes to the highest and best that is within us, when the passions come under the rule of the divine, when the life of the flesh yields to the life of the Spirit. It has been said that there is only one question each of us must decide: "Which, of the two persons that you necessarily are, do you most deeply want to perish in order that the other might wear the crown?" In William James's famed definition there also is this insight. In conversion, he says, the divided self "becomes unified . . . in consequence of its firmer hold upon religious realities." Being born again is not just finding an integrative philosophy of life; it is responding affirmatively to the highest that we know and doing this in relationship to a transcendent reality—God.

Shakespeare wrote: "What a piece of work is man! How noble in reason! How infinite in faculty! In form and moving how admirable! In action how like an angel! In apprehension how like a god! The beauty of the world—the paragon of animals!"

A few short years after Shakespeare's death, however, Blaise Pascal was born. In a dramatic phrase he emphasized another aspect of human nature. He wrote: " . . . man, . . . what a monster, what chaos, what a subject of contradiction, what a prodigy! Judge of all things, yet an imbecile earthworm: depository of truth, yet a sewer of uncertainty and error: pride and refuse of the universe."

To our detriment, we sometimes overlook this aspect of our nature. Our pride prevents us from looking at the harsh reality. It is one of the astonishing facts of our time that at the very point in history where we have been faced with the horrors of gas chambers, atomic destruction, and the liquidation of masses, we not only refuse to acknowledge the enormity of human evil but seriously entertain distortedly optimistic estimates of humankind.

The Apostle Paul speaks to this situation by affirming, "There is no distinction; since all have sinned and fall short of the glory of God" (Romans 3:23). Here, then, is the *second* thing we must consider about humankind. The Bible and Christian tradition say we are fallen creatures. There was a time when our understanding of sin was embedded in a theology which spoke of Adam and Eve as the parents of the human race who lived in a state of innocence, but their disobedience involved all of humankind in a separation from God. When the scientists came along with theories about human evolutionary development, this seemed to dispel the old notions of a fall.

In our generation, however, theologians have rediscovered "original sin." They no longer optimistically predict our inevitable rise to perfection. Our inhumanity to one another has too clearly documented depths of evil and currents of rebellion within each of us.

The psychologists add their word of confirmation. They say we are whirlpools of unresolved conflict. Just as most of an iceberg is hidden beneath the surface of the water, so most of our behavior finds its wellsprings beneath the surface of our awareness. Residual in each of us is a vast set of contradictions, struggles, and unresolved tensions which occasionally erupt. Little wonder that the existentialists, whose philosophy so dominated our thought for two decades, should speak of the human race as unpredictable and unreliable.

The dramatists in recent years have contributed their description of our condition. And they are convinced that there is a depravity about us that thwarts our best intentions. Arthur Miller's "After the Fall" describes our condition as a sequel to some mythic fall. The central character, in spite of his good intentions, had spoiled his own life and the lives of those involved with him. He was weighed down with a sense of his own pointlessness. He had fallen away from a divine intention, and this is the root of the human tragedy.

Christian faith makes clear that the human condition is not what it ought to be, what God intended it to be. Something is seriously wrong. A strong word is needed to describe it. That word is *sin*. The Bible and Christian tradition say that we are sinners estranged from God.

Every thoughtful person is aware of the paradox of human wretchedness and greatness. We can rise to the heights; we can descend to the depths. There is inward tension, contradiction, and conflict. We are jungles of inward turmoil and ambivalence. This pull between the two forces creates the dynamic of movement out of which growth and renewal can come. The *third* thing, therefore, that we must say about human nature is that it is in tension, never standing still, always in the process of becoming. Paul Tournier, the Swiss psychotherapist, writes: ". . . . man in movement, continually undergoing change, a man living in history, unfolding from his birth until his death." For a long period the approach to the study of humankind was static. Modern psychology and Christian theology both affirm, however, that we are in movement, but the direction is open.

Do you remember Kipling's great classic entitled "Letting the Jungle In"? It is the story of a group of people who went into the jungle, made a cleared place, brought their stock, planted their crops, and built their homes. For awhile it was a veritable paradise, until the rain years came and the jungle crept back. Wild animals killed their stock. The prolific vegetation of the jungle moved in faster than they could cope with it. The jungle took back their paradise. Of course, Kipling wasn't writing about the jungle at all. He was writing about humankind. He knew how near the jungle lies to the settlements of men and women, how thin is the veneer of civilization and how deep the savage in us. Our great upset at home and abroad today is but further evidence that Kipling was right. Today the beast, the jungle, our savage nature have suddenly begun to emerge again and it looks as if the jungle is about to take over again.

The meaning of the New Testament is that God has given us the help to turn back the jungle. John wrote, "all who received him . . . he gave power to become children of God" (1:12). We cannot conquer our perverse nature without divine help. There are those who, in moments of personal triumph, throw out the chest and shout, "I am the captain of my soul!" They believe salvation is for the weaklings. For a time this may work. But soon this make-believe world fades. And we are back to the same struggle which faced the Apostle Paul: There is a "warring . . . in my members" (KJV).

T. Z. Koo, one of the great Chinese Christian leaders in the early part of this century, has often told what won him to Christianity in his student days. It was simply that Christianity came to him with a proposition different from that offered by any other religion. Confucianism, in which he grew up, was concerned only with ethics, only with the right and wrong of things, but Dr. Koo says that he did not find peace by simply trying to be a good man. In fact, the persistent sense of failure made him more wretched.

Then he heard about Christ, a Personality, who could enter life. He became a Christian, and to his surprise the ethical program followed. As he stood in a new relationship to God, the old discouraging cry of "I ought" and "I must" was changed to the redeeming "I can" and "I will." When we are empowered by Christ, then we enter the realm of moral possibility.

This brings us to the *fourth* biblical statement about humanity: "Therefore, if any one is in Christ, he is a new creation" (2 Corinthians 5:17*a*). This is the heart of the matter. A Harlem pastor says, "I shudder when I hear Christians talk about meeting the real needs of men and then go on to list everything short of spiritual regeneration." God has acted in Christ to "break the power of cancelled sin" and restore us to a right relationship with himself. Leonard Griffith writes: "Christianity has added a new rung to the ladder of evolution. Christianity has produced on this earth a new creature who lives in a new way to which the natural man can no more attain than a crawling thing can fly; a creature whose way of life is so radically different from what it has left behind that we can describe it by no other term than 'rebirth.' So if the question be asked objectively, 'How can a man be born when he is old?' it can be answered objectively, 'He is born through friendship with Jesus Christ.' "

The new birth is something more than a resolve, which needs repeated reenforcement, to respond to the greater good. It is the awareness that we are incapable of pulling ourselves up by our own goodness to approach unto God. Jesus went to the cross to make it clear that salvation is of God; we are forgiven and renewed and acceptable to God because of his action. This is the meaning of the parable of the prodigal son.

One year during the Lenten season I went to see a drama that portrayed the life of Jesus. "The Man Born to Be King" reached its climax in the crucifixion scene. The three Marys entered and approached the Roman guards. Mary, the mother of Jesus, spoke to the captain requesting permission to minister to the needs of her Son. He roughly pushed her away. Then one of the other women came forward and sought permission, adding: "For old times' sake." The guard refused her request. Then with a sweeping motion of her hand she loosed her golden hair so it could cascade down her back. "Marcellus," she asked, "have you ever seen hair like this?" And then she thrust out a foot and asked, "and have feet ever danced for you as these feet?"

Incredulity was on his face. In amazement he said: "Mary Magdalene, how you have changed!" Slowly, with dramatic emphasis, she turned so her back was to the audience and she was facing the cross and slowly said: "Yes, Marcellus, I have changed; he changed me."

This is what the new birth means. It means that all of us who were once aliens from divine favor can be accepted by a loving God as revealed in a cross. We can be released from the bondage of pretense and sin and become the persons God intends us to be. We are changed through accepting Christ as the One who reconciles God and humanity—the One who by his forgiving grace overcomes our estrangement.

Commitment

To acknowledge Jesus as our Lord is to affirm that we belong to him. He is to rule in life. For years Augustine prayed that he might turn from his pagan ways and become a Christian. He even prayed, "Make me chaste." But he was living with a concubine, and his will always added to the prayer, "but not now." New birth cannot take place when we consciously withhold areas of life from the control of Christ. To the rich young ruler Jesus said that he must rid himself of the lesser god in his life—his possessions—and surrender self to the lordship of Christ.

The tragedy of modern life is not in its absurdity but in the absurd way in which we rebel against the commitment of ourselves to Christ. Saying *yes* to him is the conscious yielding of the whole self to God. No one would suggest this is an accomplishment easily achieved, but how foolish not to do so!

Self-assertion demands that we save ourselves through our own efforts rather than through surrender. The source of our salvation, however, is the universal atonement of Jesus Christ, and the channel by which the effects of this are brought to us is our faith. Both are merciful, undeserved gifts from God to the one who in humble repentance and believing faith says *yes* to Christ. This does not mean that every person will pass through an identical sort of experience, but whatever his or her experience, each person will be a true Christian.

In the middle of his life the great Russian, Leo Tolstoi, wrote, "Five years ago I came to believe in Christ and my life suddenly changed. I ceased to desire what I had previously desired and began to desire what I formerly did not want. . . . The direction of my life and my desires became different, and good and evil changed places."

How does all this happen? For some there is a sudden, spectacular experience which the embryologists call "condensed evolution." It is also true, however, that some of the most lasting, earth-shaking Christian conversions have taken place quietly, almost imperceptibly and over a long period of time, so that only in retrospect, only by looking back, as you look down a mountain to see how far you have climbed, do you realize the extent of the change in your life. How it happens we do not know except to say, God must do it.

John Wesley spoke of prevenient grace. Because of original sin, we are dead to God and unable to move toward, or respond to God. It is through prevenient grace that we are given the power to respond or resist. Only as God moves within our lives do we have the power to accept faith or refuse it.

The greatest of all the affirmative verses in the Bible is John 3:16: "God so loved . . . that he gave." This is the clue to how God brings about the change in human nature.

CHAPTER NINE

SACRAMENTS

he Doctrinal Statement defines the church as "the sacramental community when, by adoration, proclamation, and self-sacrifice its members become conformed to Christ. Persons are initiated and incorporated into this community of faith by baptism and confirmation and accept their membership as confirmed by the Holy Spirit. By continuing celebration of the Lord's Supper, or Holy Communion, the church participates in the risen and present Body of Christ, being thereby nourished and strengthened by faithful discipleship. With churches of many traditions, United Methodists affirm baptism and the Lord's Supper as the *two* principal sacraments given by God to his people."

The Roman Catholic Church, however, gives sacramental significance to seven of the many religious acts which were practiced in the early church—Baptism, Confirmation, the Holy Eucharist, Penance, Extreme Unction, Orders, and Matrimony. By way of contrast, the Quakers believe that the grace of God is immediate in the heart and feel no need for ritual acts as means of grace.

Important as we feel the sacraments are to the Christian faith, it is well to remember that God cannot be limited and may work with or without them. The clergy must be careful lest they take themselves and the fact of whether or not one has received, for instance, tangible baptism too seriously. By this, of course, we mean the mechanical rite itself, not the fruit it produces. John Wesley stated it well in his *Letters*, III, 36: "You think the mode of baptism is 'necessary to salvation.' I deny that even baptism itself is so; if it were, every Quaker must be damned, which I can in no wise believe. I hold nothing to be (strictly speaking) necessary to salvation but the mind which was in Christ."

Nevertheless, baptism and the Lord's Supper have been a part of the life of the Christian church since they were instituted by Jesus. The objects used in the sacraments all belong to the common life—water, bread, wine—but they set before us great unseen realities. As means of conveying God's grace, as symbols of God's creative and redemptive power and as memorials of what God has done for us through Jesus Christ, we do believe they are central to our life and faith.

What is a sacrament? It suggests something mysterious, beyond human understanding and knowledge, something sacred. The word itself, incidentally, comes from the Latin word "sacramentum" and was the word given to a sum deposited by two parties to a suit. Thus it suggests a covenant between God and persons and has become, in the practice of the church, that formal moment when we celebrate the mystery of God and the covenantal relationship to those whom God created. It is, therefore, a dramatic reminder that God has done something: it is finished, accomplished. It is a symbol of creative, redemptive power. We are reminded God has acted in our behalf. It is also an instrument through which God is now doing something. The action continues. Finally, in United Methodist understanding the effectiveness of the sacrament depends for its final fulfillment upon our doing something.

We turn now to an examination of the first idea that a sacrament is a reminder that God has acted in our behalf, has done something which is completed. The bread and wine say: "God's love has been sacrificially expressed in your behalf." Christ died on the cross for the sins of the world, and that includes you. It need not be done again. It was accomplished. Baptism reminds us that God granted the Holy Spirit for our renewal, cleansing, and transformation and established the church into which we may be incorporated. The sacraments, or ordinances, give visible assurance of God's presence and serve as signs of the divine initiative taken in the realm of our redemption. The divine acts form the objective element. God has acted, regardless of our response.

The sacraments are not only dramatic reminders of what God has done, but they are, in the second place, vehicles and instruments through which God is now doing something. They are pictures and symbols reminding us that God is coming to us now with forgiveness and saving help. In the Book of Acts there is no clear pattern, but it is plain that baptism was closely connected with the gift of the Spirit. Alone or with "Confirmation," it brought the gift. John 3:5 says,

"Unless one is born of water and the Spirit, [one] cannot enter the kingdom of God." It is impossible to state definitely whether the writer wishes to stress either of the two media, to the implied detriment if not the exclusion of the other, or whether he wishes to stress the necessity of both media. It would seem that "water and the Spirit" is one phrase which would suggest this is the way the early church understood baptism. If this is true, then baptism is thought of primarily as the gateway of the new birth. Something is happening now.

Baptism

In this view the center of gravity is on rebirth to a spiritual life rather than on a remembered identification with Christ in his death and resurrection. Paul hints at this in 1 Corinthians 6:11 when he says of the Corinthian Christians, "You were washed, you were sanctified, you were justified in the name of the Lord Jesus Christ and in the Spirit of our God." For Paul, baptism was "into Christ," into union with him, into possession by him, into all the benefits, e.g., justification and sanctification, which flowed from being linked to him. Union with Christ involved sharing in his death and resurrection, of which baptism was an obvious sign and symbol. The Messianic age had dawned, and both Jew and Gentile could enter it by faith, the proof and expression of which was the acceptance of baptism. There was a new creature in a new creation. Baptism initiated converts into an organism. Thoughts such as these, particularly those associated with death and resurrection, suggest that baptism moved in the same circle of ideas as the Eucharist. Both were sacraments of union with Christ, leading to union with and in Christ's body. One was the sacrament of initiation; the other of continuing fellowship. The stress was on what it did for the believer now.

Compared with other church traditions in United Methodism, baptism as an external and visible act is given a secondary place and stress is laid on repentance, conversion, and justification, rather than on sacramental acts. This may reflect our heritage, coming from the revival movement, and emphasizing the personal conduct of the individual church member. It is significant, for instance, that Wesley in his amended version of the Thirty-Nine Articles of Religion replaced Article XVI "Of Sin After Baptism" by "Of Sin After Justification" (Article XII). This emphasis is reflected in the questions put to adults at the time of baptism: "Do you truly and earnestly repent of your sins and accept Jesus Christ as your Savior?" and "Will you obediently keep God's holy will and commandments and walk in the same all the days of your life?"

When the candidate has answered these questions, the pastor then addresses the congregation: " . . . Will you endeavor so to live that this person may grow in the knowledge and love of God the Father through our Lord Jesus Christ?" and the congregation is to respond: "With God's help we will so order our lives after the example of Christ that, surrounded by steadfast love, you may be established in the faith, and confirmed and strengthened in the way that leads to life eternal." These questions show the importance, in United Methodism, attached to admission and integration into the community of the faithful. In fact, the introductory statement of the minister is an invitation to the congregation to pray that God, "of his bounteous goodness will grant unto this person (that he/she) may receive the forgiveness of sins, be baptized with water and the Holy Spirit, and may be received into Christ's holy Church, and be made a living member of the same."

In other words, it is an act of dedication to God's will and purpose for our lives. It is also an act of initiation, by which we are grafted to the Body of Christ. It is, in summary, an act of spiritual new life and an identification with Christ's death and resurrection.

The third idea is our conviction that the effectiveness depends upon our doing something. We do not insist upon any one form of baptism. There are three principal modes: sprinkling, pouring, and immersion. Every adult and the parents of every child to be baptized have the choice. The reason for this flexibility is our belief that the amount of water used is not important. There was a time in Christian history when baptism was thought to have magical powers. The water was believed to have regenerating power of itself, if it had been consecrated by ritualistic words and made "holy water." From our point of view, the application of water does not change the nature of a person. It is easy to lapse into superstition. Parents who want a child baptized, but never attend church or teach the Christian faith in the home, illustrate this. Nor can the application of water remove the curse of our sin and impart a new nature and character. An ocean of water cannot effect a spiritual change. No sacred words or symbolic acts can make a person a disciple. Mode, in our judgment, and again stressing the subjective, is not as important as meaning and faith. We do not believe that the water has the power either to save or to damn. What the act does depends upon the inward response.

As one of our leaders reminds us, "Baptism is not the new birth, it is not regeneration, but it does save us, it does start us on the road to sanctification: if we repent, if we live in response to Christ's claim upon our lives, if we believe with heart, soul, mind, and strength, and if we obey the gospel's demand upon our lives. But if these assumptions and expectations are not fulfilled, then our baptism is not valid and has no saving power in itself." What we are trying to say is that the sacraments are one of the means by which God comes to us with forgiveness and saving help but freedom is at the heart of it. There is nothing coercive. It is finally a free meeting of spirit with Spirit. God comes with grace and help but we must respond in faith and obedience. Even in infant baptism the child must finally claim for himself or herself the covenant relationship with God if the relationship is to be sealed and made complete.

The validity of the sacrament depends, finally, upon the inward response to the outward symbol. Preaching does not save the world else the world would have been saved long ago. A sermon saves in the measure that hearers respond to the message by applying it to their own lives. And so with baptism. We read in the Gospel that except a person be born of water and the spirit, that person cannot enter the kingdom of God. Water alone does not save, but if accompanied by an earnest resolution to live a Christ-committed life, baptism can be a means of grace.

Then, you may ask, why do we baptize infants? Because if baptism is recognition of membership in the family of God, then it is natural for parents to want their children to receive this sign of being a part of God's kingdom. And by this act they acknowledge their thanksgiving for child life, they dedicate the child to the plan and purpose of God, and they vow to rear the youngster in the nurture of the faith so that when arriving at the years of discretion the child will be able to make the response of faith.

No church, to my knowledge, that baptizes infants, makes baptism equivalent to church membership. There is a second ceremony, known as confirmation, when at a later age the baptized person reaffirms the vow his or her parents took on his or her behalf at baptism. Every denomination that baptizes has two requirements for church membership: baptism and the taking of vows of discipleship. The churches that emphasize adult baptism meet the two requirements at the same time.

As to the further meanings of infant baptism, we do not view this as creating a new condition. We do not teach that the nature of the child is so polluted that if the youngster should die he or she would be lost forever. We are reluctant to suggest that baptism is a cleansing from the corruption of original sin.

Neither is it just a sweet ceremony. There is something about a child that attracts attention. Brides are often cautioned when planning a wedding that if they have a flower girl they must accept the fact that the youngster will probably receive more attention than the bride! And when parents present a child in a service of worship for the sacrament of baptism, every eye is directed toward the youngster. Baptism, however, is much more than a sweet and sentimental occasion. For this reason we suggest that this important sacrament not be sentimentalized by the use of a flower dipped into water and placed on the infant's head. This has no historic significance and cannot take the place of the hand of the pastor placed directly upon the infant's head as a symbol that life is lived under the care and providence of God. As has been suggested, "We are dealing here with a profound spiritual mystery, not a touching ceremony."

One United Methodist theologian has summarized the cause of infant baptism by saying we observe this practice "because by birth God has set his mark and seal on each little child and claimed him for himself and his people." Because God's mighty redemptive work in Jesus Christ has already been done in behalf of each infant, the church celebrates that fact. Again, we believe in infant baptism because the whole community of faith, along with the family, needs to lift up each little child and claim him or her for Christ and the church in advance of the age of accountability. In all things, including religion, the infant goes with the family.

The ritual reminds us that infant baptism is "an outward and visible sign of the grace of the Lord Jesus Christ, through which grace we become partakers of his righteousness and heirs of life eternal." The child presented in baptism is acknowledged as a part of the kingdom of love and care.

"Those receiving the sacrament are thereby marked as Christian disciples, and initiated into the fellowship of Christ's Holy Church. Our Lord has expressly given to little children a place among the people of God." This is what our liturgy and practice affirm.

We baptize children recognizing that of such is the kingdom of God, and that they are already a part of God's kingdom of love and care and are entitled to baptism which is the outward sign.

We are all God's children by birth. Baptism is the visible witness of this in the face of an often forgetful world. Baptism does not make a person a child of God, but it is a public declaration of the fact that one is already a child of God.

The coronation did not make Elizabeth II the monarch of Britain, for coronation can only make a person a sovereign who is a sovereign already. It is the public declaration of a fact which already existed. A nation says: "This person is of royal lineage—put the crown on her head." The church says: "This person is a child of God—baptize him or her."

It is also an opportunity for parents to dramatize their faith that they believe their child is not only physical and mental but spiritual and they have a responsibility to care for all aspects of the child's nature. The question they are asked reads: "Do you therefore accept as your bounden duty and privilege to live before this child a life that becomes the Gospel (and) will you endeavor to keep this child under the ministry and guidance of the Church until he by the power of God shall accept for himself the gift of salvation and be confirmed as a full and responsible member of Christ's Holy Church?"

They, the sponsors, and the Christian community, are confessing a responsibility for the spiritual nurture of this youngster in the devout hope and expectation that when able, the child will "take for himself or herself" a measure of responsibility for a deepening relationship with God.

There are those, of course, who raise questions about the authority for baptizing infants,. Certainly the Bible does not command it or forbid it. It is a practice that grew up very early in the church. While probably it did not become universal until later—the first church was principally an adult church—there are references in the New Testament even to men and women baptized with their "households" (Acts 16:15,33; 1 Corinthians 1:16), which certainly would not exclude children. During the second century, the Church Fathers referred to the practice of infant baptism as "apostolic" and to those who "had been made disciples from childhood." But whatever the weight of scriptural evidence or early practice, it is appropriate that parents and the believing community should want their children baptized in recognition of their place in the family of God. And the church could not refuse them, when our Lord took "the little ones" in his arms and blessed them (Mark 10:16). Also, as someone suggested, it is good wisdom to start the child right, in the company of Christ and his followers. Dramatic though the rescue of prodigals may be, it is better in the economy of the kingdom for the children never to leave the Father's house. Baptism is preventive medicine at the spiritual level.

The Lord's Supper

The sacrament of the Lord's Supper is just as rich in meaning as baptism but more easily understood in United Methodist practice. It relates, of course, to the last supper which Jesus ate with his disciples (1 Corinthians 11:23-25). In the early church, before the ceremonial rite celebrated apart from the meal had developed, the followers of Christ met to have a meal together in memory of the event. They called it the *love-feast*, a term which reminded them of the warmth of their fellowship in Christ. Much of this idea is suggested by our present word *communion*. When we say "holy communion" we are recognizing its sacredness. In some denominations it is called the "Eucharist" which means thanksgiving, from the thanks which Jesus expressed when he took the bread and the cup in the Last Supper.

The Last Supper is a sacrament by which God comes to us reminding us of what has been done in the gift of the only begotten Son. It is a memorial service. The whole story of his suffering, death, and resurrection for our sakes is brought to our attention. "My body . . . given for you . . . do this in remembrance." United Methodists tend to stress the memorial aspects, the remembering, the recollection of Jesus.

It is also a time when God is doing something within us. The invitation calls for repentance from sin, an expression of love toward our neighbors, and the will to lead a new life according to the commandments of God. This call to repentance is followed by confession and a petition for forgiveness.

We do not believe that by some physical miracle the bread and wine have become the actual body and blood of Christ. We must not neglect the emphasis, however, that Christ was given for our sins. In receiving the elements of remembrance, we can enter then into the newness of life. That is why there is a stress on confession, penitence, and dedication. As the drama of Christ's death and the assurance of his loving presence are reenacted, lives can be quickened, and our wills renewed. As one of our United Methodist theologians reminds us, "Through the bread and wine and symbolic acts, the death of Christ ceases to be merely past history and becomes a present, saving power in the lives of the worshipers."

There is also a rich quality of fellowship inherent in the practice of this sacrament. It is not a solitary act, it is "communion." We have fellowship with the disciples, martyrs, and the fathers of the faith. We do not believe in the "cafeteria concept" where worshipers come alone and help themselves. This sacrament is a visible, meaningful sign instituted by Christ and performed by the historical church acting through recognized ministers or by agents who intend to act for the church. You might distribute to your own family broken bread and the fruit of the vine and it would have rich devotional significance, but for the sacramental character to be recognized we feel that the qualities of the church and recognized agents who act for the church must be present forming that link with the "choir invisible."

There is also a recognition that we must be in love and charity with our neighbors. Taking bread together can give us a sense of fellowship. This is not only with the person in the pew but with those who are followers of the Christ all around the world. This is why we frequently take an offering for "others" on "World-wide Communion Sunday." We are made to think of that great company of Christians of all ages who have remembered the Christ. It gives us a lifting sense of the reality of the "communion of saints."

Included in this fellowship is our doctrine of the "real presence" of Christ. When we come to the table of the Lord in the Spirit of Christ, we find him there. "Do this in remembrance of me" and he is there. "Lo, I am with you always" is the rich promise. What a beautiful sight it is to see Christian people kneeling together, receiving the elements, and in deep communion with their fellow-believers all over the world, and with the Christ.

There is one more aspect of this sacrament that needs to be mentioned. It is a reminder that all life is sacramental. When we use the common elements of bread, the staff of life, and the fruit of the vine which in Jesus' day was the common drink, we are saying that all life is sacramental. The common things of life can be used as symbols of the spiritual. The world about us can be the instrument by which God comes to us. The humble tasks in which all of us engage as we go about our daily round should be the links which bind us to God. And in this spirit we can, while kneeling at the sacrament, offer our lives to God each day.

CHAPTER TEN

PRAYER

 nited Methodists have always stressed the personal, the subjective, the experiential. We believe in person-to-person communion with God. We believe it is possible to have a genuine awareness of the greatness, glory, mystery, and love of God. This is based on our conviction that God, the Creator and Sustainer, is approachable. Our Doctrinal Statement affirms "Life in the Spirit means . . . the life of prayer and inward searching; it also involves . . . the communal life of the church." When Wesley formed the societies he defined their purpose by saying a society is no other than "a company of men having the form and seeking the power of godliness, united in order to pray together, to receive the word of exhortation, and to watch over one another in love, that they may help each other to work out their salvation." He also spoke of the "ordinances of God" which included "family and private prayer."

Many things are hard to explain. One of these is prayer. At best our explanations are halting and awkward. We don't, however, omit prayer because we can't understand its full meaning. Jesus himself demonstrated this in his use of prayer. He made no effort to argue or analyze the subject. As he assumed the existence of God, so he also assumed the naturalness of prayer. He did not raise or answer the problems which weigh so heavily upon educated persons today. He lived in an age when nearly all people believed in prayer and most practiced at least the outward forms. But our generation does not take prayer as seriously. There may be many reasons.

Perhaps prayer is dismissed because of the overpowering influence of secularism. In a world of scientific certainty and mathematical probability, why pray? As one young college student said, "Science does not deny God; it goes one better; it makes God unnecessary!" It could be that we have ceased to believe in a God who pays attention to prayer. Another person writes: "Surely no responsible person any longer believes that it is possible to know or experience God in anything that is genuinely modern."

Attitudes

To pray effectively requires certain attitudes. We must first believe that prayer has value. Alfred Lord Tennyson once wrote that "more things are wrought by prayer than this world dreams of."

Does prayer really make a difference, or is it just good therapy? The Apostle James wrote, "The prayer of a righteous man has great power in its effects" (James 5:16). In the very next verse he says, "Elijah was a man of like nature with ourselves and he prayed fervently that it might not rain, and for three years and six months it did not rain on the earth. Then he prayed again and the heaven gave rain. . . ." Take special note of the phrase, "a man of like nature with ourselves." But an examination of his life reveals that when he had a need, he knew that God was the source of supply. He then prayed earnestly. He prayed in faith, and an answer came. Effectual prayer involves a conviction that it has limitless possibilities for renewal, guidance, and power. No one will pray without the conviction that it can make a difference.

The second necessary attitude is the conviction that there is an interior life which must be cultivated. General Charles de Gaulle was quoted as saying, "Man wants to travel to the moon. That is not far enough. He must first travel to the depths of his own soul." There is an echo in that phrase of the scriptural passage which says, "For what shall it profit a man, if he shall gain the whole world and lose his own soul?" (Mark 8:36, KJV).

The great discoveries of the next decades will hopefully be in the mental and spiritual realm. This is our only hope for remaining truly human, for if our spiritual advances don't keep pace with our technology, then we are doomed! We must develop, sensitize, and strengthen life's inner resources. The late C. G. Jung, a one-time disciple of Freud, said that the individual who is not anchored in God can offer no resistance of his or her own resources to the physical and moral blandishments of the world. Only as we have concluded that "we cannot live by bread alone" will we devote the necessary energy and effort the spiritual cultivation requires. It is, however, the great imperative of our generation.

The third required attitude is a firm conviction that the theistic position is valid. By this I simply mean a belief, rooted in faith and experience, that God is personally interested in what happens to us and will not abandon that which has been created.

The Christian faith has always taught that prayer is a two-way communication between ourselves and the God whom Jesus came to reveal and to serve, and it must be stated as clearly as possible that unless one does believe in God, there is nothing left to say about prayer. Prayer is not talking to ourselves; it is not simply cajoling ourselves into a better frame of mind. It is standing on the solid ground of God's omnipotent goodness.

Piety, Action, and Intercession

Let us now examine the three major dimensions of prayer as understood by United Methodists. *First*, it is private, personal, and mystical. It is the ascent leading toward the vision of God. It is communion with the Creator, Sustainer, and Empowerer of our lives. It is receiving the blessings and benefits which God has for us.

This private aspect is accomplished in many ways. It is reading and reflecting on the Word of God. The spiritual masters have a disciplined pattern of time and place for the encounter with God. We may not have this, but all of us can use the moments of solitude that present themselves for reflection and brooding. The word *brooding* has a bad image. It connotes a low-grade distemper, meditative melancholy, the power of negative thinking. But this is unfair to brooding, which, as any hen knows, can be a most productive experience. It's the sort of "sitting on an idea" that often yields fresh insight. It's the kind of fruitful pondering one may do in the solitude of early morning or late evening, or when protected by the anonymity of a commuter train or bus. This thought, coming from a book by Robert Raines, *Creative Brooding*, reminds us that all around are selections from newspapers, magazines, plays, poets, and the Bible, which can be used for reflection and prayer. Such reflection should shake the foundations, awake thought, and precipitate action.

Marcus Aurelius once observed that weak persons seek retreats, whereas strong persons carry theirs with them. To nurture within oneself a resource to turn to—a place to go—toughens the fiber and expands the horizons of the human spirit. Self-pitying isolation must be avoided, but creative aloneness provides an essential place of rest and renewal on our journey toward worthy selfhood. There is no cure for self-centered loneliness comparable to a life shared with the Eternal.

Another thing we can do is use our imagination. The mind is active all the time. The imagination moves in many directions. Cultivate the habit of making it work for you. In Mark 11:24 we read, "Whatever you ask in prayer, believe that you have received it, and it will be yours." The Bible also reminds us that the thoughts of a person characterize the person. All this suggests the importance of the mind and imagination.

Many psychologists regard the imagination as more powerful than the will. They believe that if the will is set in one direction but the imagination is firmly held in another, the imagination will ultimately win. Employ the imagination in prayer. Picture yourself already possessing the graces you desire. Picture the prayer fulfilled. Link imagination with affirmation. Hold in your mind the image of yourself made anew in Christ. See it with clarity and conviction. See the fearful you, truly trusting—the resentful you, fully forgiving.

Someone has said that all of us carry on a constant dialogue with ourselves. We shall be reluctant to place too much emphasis upon the "power of positive thinking," but there is truth here that can be ignored only at our own risk. We know there is power in negative thinking. "As a person thinks, so is he." There is power in these words. So think the best, the highest, the noblest, about yourself and others for such thoughts, such imaginations, have a way of becoming self-fulfilling.

We must realize, of course, that prayer as communion with God is much more than reflection or the creative use of the imagination. This may suggest how we can creatively use available resources for praying, but it is also a "person-to-person" communion with God. It is a meeting of "Spirit with spirit." What this is cannot be adequately defined or described. It must be experienced.

The late Harry Emerson Fosdick, in his autobiography, tells that when he was a young preacher he suffered a severe nervous break-down. This was followed by a period of bitter depression. "For the first time in my life," he wrote, "I faced, at my wit's end, a situation too much for me to handle. I went down into the depths where self-confidence becomes ludicrous. . . . In that experience I learned some things about religion that theological seminaries do not teach. I learned to pray, not because I had adequately argued out prayer's rationality, but because I desperately needed help from a Power greater than my own. I learned that God, much more than a the-ological proposition, is an immediately available Resource." What an exciting discovery to make!

The *second* dimension of prayer for us is the linking of piety with social action. Before leaping into the battle to correct injustice, we should gain the "mind of Christ." When we understand that we are doing Christ's work, we have a sustaining motivational power.

A little girl came home from school with pride over what she had learned that day. She was eager to tell someone. "Daddy," she exclaimed eagerly, "I learned what the earth does every twenty-four hours." "What does it do, honey?" dutifully asked her father. "It revolts on its abscess," was the quick answer. A sickness has laid its hands upon our world. Needs are so urgent. There is so much to do. And people of prayer must also act.

The venerable Albert Schweitzer, in his declining years, was asked by a reporter about the world's distress. Schweitzer shared with him his philosophy: "No matter how great the evil of the world, I always hold firmly to the conviction that each of us can do something to bring some portion of that evil to an end." Our prayer should be, "Lord, show me what I can do about the world's evil."

Piety without social concern is incomplete. When Francis of Assisi prayed for the lepers of Italy, it occurred to him that God expected him to do more than pray, so he went and lived with them. He lavished care upon them, dressed their wounds, and became one with them in their sufferings.

One of our greatest assets in the struggle with evil is to live a life of faith and integrity. This confirms our witness for truth and equity. We need to pray about our decisions. God will make available to the inner consciousness a wisdom greater than our own. God's will, will be made known to us if we wait and listen. Preachers tell an old story of a pastor who was invited to another church at a considerable increase in salary. He did not know if he should go and was devoting much time to prayer. One day a parishioner saw his small son on the sidewalk and asked what his daddy was going to do. The youngster replied, "Well, Father's praying, but Mother's packing!" In many of our decisions the desire for reward, the fear of punishment, or the love of self intrudes and prevents the accomplishment of God's will. We need divine wisdom as we try to make decisions and render choices.

We need to pray about the moral sag in life. Jesus recognized that we struggle with evil. He spoke of temptation. He noted that we often need to pray for forgiveness. All of us need strength to resist the wrong.

The *third* dimension of prayer for United Methodists grows out of our conviction that we should pray for others. We do believe in intercessory prayer. Jesus prayed for others. By example, Jesus taught his disciples to pray for each other. Paul and others persisted in this practice. Every church should have intercessory prayer groups who lift the needs of each other, and of the world, to the throne of God's mercy. "No man is an Iland, intire of it selfe," John Donne reminds us. Each person is a part of the mainland of humanity, a member of the human family, an integral part of the divine-human community. As such, we are all related to others and depend upon others for our very existence.

This sense of being related to others gives validity to our prayers. Dr. Edward Bauman writes:

> When we pray for others we are holding their lives up before God so that his light may shine upon them. We are seeking to influence them to open their lives to God. In turn, we are strengthened by the prayers of others in our moments of deepest distress. This mutual influence, which comes from prayer, is similar to other influences arising out of the social nature of our existence. Such prayer helps to break down the barriers that separate men from one another, barriers that often lead to increased misunderstanding. Modern science and industry have done a great deal to overcome barriers of time and distance, but many people still face each other across formidable obstacles of race and religion, of interest and education, of ideas and ideals.

Unable to communicate and cooperate because of such obstacles, persons often find themselves unwillingly involved in incidents of hatred and bloodshed. How different the situation is when men are sincerely praying for one another! William Law emphasized this value of intercession in strengthening community relationships when he said, "There is nothing that makes us love a man so much as praying for him."

Praying is sometimes all we can do for one another. Frank Laubach, the literacy expert, dedicated a book with these words: "To all who are dissatisfied with what they are doing for the world." If we feel discontent that we cannot do more about world problems, then let us pray!

Actually, we have a sacred responsibility at this point. We often cite our Protestant heritage with its magnificent phrase, "The priesthood of all believers." This does not just mean that we have the privilege of approaching God directly. It means that the priest's approach to God is made on behalf of others. With the privilege of being a priest comes the sacred responsibility of practicing that priesthood in order to bring others into the light of God's love. So even though we are tied down by responsibilities in home and business, or weakened through sickness and disability, we can still pray. Every shut-in can still have a ministry. No person is too busy to deny himself or herself this ministry of prayer. All must practice their "priesthood" which means intercession for others. But we may appropriately ask how intercession for another "works." One suggestion is found in the development of an idea by the late Leslie Weatherhead. He has written:

Telepathy is the communication of ideas from one mind to another without the use of the senses. In my opinion, the evidence for it is conclusive. It seems to me a fact that in certain circumstances minds which are on the same "wave-length," and especially when they are under the stress of some benign emotion, do at times communicate messages to one another, geographical distance making no difference.

What beauteous insight we have here. When Paul said, "We have not ceased to pray for you," this may have been in part what he had in mind. We can touch another person on the unconscious level. And isn't this what a group is doing when they pray for another?

We certainly do not wish to imply that prayer is only telepathy. This would be the same mistake of an earlier generation who felt that evolution negated the idea of God's creative power. Actually, all evolution does is describe the creative process. In similar fashion, telepathy only describes the mental machinery by which God uses, in some cases, our intercession for our friends.

Praying for people has always puzzled us. We pray for one person, and that person recovers. We pray for another, and that person dies. The cynic might say that one person would have recovered anyway. There are no easy answers.

Christians, however, will continue to pray, for they are under command. "He told them a parable to the effect that they ought always to pray and not lose heart" (Luke 18:1). Furthermore, Christ himself prayed for others, and we cannot refuse to follow his example. Most of us, having faced our obligation to pray for others, seek some guidance and instruction as to how we proceed with this ministry of prayer. First, we are to be specific in our request—confess our needs, express our desires. Jesus did this when praying in the Garden of Gethsemane. He agonized, "Remove this cup from me" (Luke 22:42).

Make clear what we desire. "Man tells what he desires," says Luther. "He is not abashed before exalted Majesty, but speaks outright." John Calvin believed that prayer was instituted in order that "we may confess our needs to God and bring him our complaints as children bring their grievances confidently to their parents."

Then we must always make these requests, however specific, in the spirit and name of Christ who prayed, "Thy will be done." There are many times when we have wanted something very earnestly only to discover years later it would not have been to our advantage to have received our request. Our knowledge is finite and limited. Every petition must conclude with the phrase, "Thy will be done."

One of the best illustrations of how to pray is found in this incident. Howard Thurman tells of a ninety-year-old woman who had been a member of a certain church for more than fifty years. Her present pastor was not loved by the people, but he insisted on staying despite all efforts to have him removed. The woman took an entire afternoon to pray about this difficult situation. She began with the day she joined the church and unhurriedly reviewed fifty years of her own life in relation to the church. She then went into great detail, explaining to the Lord all about the pastor, the people, and the present crisis. When she finished, she said, "Now Lord, I have given you all the facts. Take them and do the best you can. I have no suggestion to make."

As we deepen our skills in prayer, we will be moved to pray less for material and temporal things and more for spiritual wishes. The Apostle Paul has given us an example of this. He asked God to give his friends such things as spiritual strength, unity, certainty, knowledge, and love. In telling them about his prayers, he reported having asked "that the name of our Lord Jesus may be glorified in you," "that you may not do wrong," "that you may be saved."

Notice the kinds of petitions Jesus offers in his intercessory prayer for his disciples. He asked the Father to "keep them in thy name." He asked that they be "sanctified in truth." He petitioned, "Don't take them out of the world, but keep them from the evil one." That is, he did not pray that the disciples would have it easy. He did pray that they would be able to withstand the evils and temptations of this present world. Gandhi said that our prayers for others should be, "Give them all the light and truth they need for their highest development."

CHAPTER ELEVEN
FAITH AND WORKS

he Doctrinal Statement says that "perhaps the most widely cherished doctrinal emphasis among United Methodists is that faith and good works belong together. Guided by the Spirit, our understanding swings between two poles. On the one side, faith is intensely personal (Christ is my 'Savior'; 'Christ for *us!*'). On the other side, as The General Rules remind us, this inward assurance, if genuine, is bound to show itself outwardly in good works. By joining heart and hand, United Methodists have stressed that personal salvation leads always to involvement in Christian mission in the world. Thus we assert that personal religion, evangelical witness, and Christian social action are reciprocal and mutually reinforcing."

One of our theologians expresses his understanding of this passage by saying, "We United Methodists continue to urge upon the contemporary world the need for the kinds of inner transformation, growth, and insight which, with the power of the Holy Spirit, necessarily issue in the responsible management of life, both personally and socially. The formula is: from inner transformation of heart and mind to creative leadership and authentic social reform." This is a splendid affirmation of the conviction that has always stood at the center of the church's teaching that faith and fruit must be linked.

The very name "Methodist" stems from the fact that Wesley and the others who shared with him in the Oxford Holy Club were "methodical" not only in the practice of their devotions but also in the accomplishment of various acts of charity, including working for penal reform. We must remember that Christianity is a materialistic religion. It is concerned with this world. Jesus prayed, "Thy will be done on earth. . . . " Christianity is not something that goes on once a week in a building we call a church. It is a way of life, a style of living. It is the total context in which we live and move and have our being. It is a way of thinking, of speaking, of acting. It has to do with home, school, community, politics, business—as well as church. The real authority of the church is an example. As an institution the church may be shorn of prestige and power. This could happen in our generation. The apostolic church, though a persecuted and dispossessed minority group, lived and grew in the power of the Holy Spirit. They were able to love one another and render no one evil. This showed the world a better way than that of hate and oppression. This proclaimed a message that survived the defeat of armies and the collapse of empires. When faith and fruit become joined, nothing can shake the church.

It is our desire to examine two questions that are urged upon us for answer. *First*, do the sacred and secular ever mix, or in practical but more emotional terms, do politics and religion ever belong together? The second question will be concerned with the prophetic role in our decade.

Politics and Religion

During the first sixteen hundred years of church history the question of mixing politics and religion would have aroused little interest because the answer would have been an obvious *yes*. In Western civilization, church and state were usually wedded. More recently, in England, Italy, Israel, Pakistan, Iran, and numerous other countries the link between state and religion is openly acknowledged.

Our own Pilgrim ancestors assumed they would be conjoined. But in time they discovered, as did John Calvin in Geneva, that a church invested with national authority can become oppressive. The witch-hunt was the more dramatic form this took in our own history.

Finally, through the efforts of many persons, notably Roger Williams, who played a role in the establishment of Rhode Island, the idea of the separation of church and state was accepted. Historians have called this the *Great Experiment*. Many of us, as youngsters working puzzles, learned the long word *antidisestablishmentarianism* which simply meant you were against separation of church and state.

By the time of the writing of the Constitution, the pluralistic character of our society was apparent; and it is a part of our national life that Congress shall make no law respecting the establishment of religion. This is not designed to be anti-religion. It means the state shall not dominate the church as it did in Nazi Germany and now in Russia, nor should the church dominate the state as it did for several centuries in Italy. Nor does it prevent the national government from being concerned about the church. We do not pay taxes on the building in which we meet for worship; clergy are exempt from the selective service.

And the church is not prevented from making its point of view known. The first amendment supports the right of citizens to "petition the government for redress of grievances." If the church officially becomes a lobby, however, it can lose its tax-exempt status. What is the situation today?

There is the attitude of complete separation. In the Sixties an organization known as "Clergymen and Laymen Concerned About Vietnam" asked pastors and laypersons to go to Washington and call on their congressional representatives. One pastor wrote to his congressman saying, "I will not be among them. I will stay at home and preach the gospel." But those who stayed home and preached the gospel had to be concerned about the welfare situation in their city, the quality of public education, the rights of minorities, and all the other issues that make for human betterment. None of us believe that preaching the gospel is just saving a soul with no concern for the quality of one's present life.

Another point of view is that the church must make its voice felt on issues that directly affect the church and its activities such as opportunity for missions, freedom of speech as it pertains to the media and evangelism, and the sending of ambassadors or envoys to the Vatican. They would insist that only when the state infringes on a citizen's responsibility to God does the citizen have the right to defy the state.

The third point of view, taken by most United Methodists, is expressed by one senator who has said, "Every political question is a moral question, which challenges politicians to seek the guidance of the church." This view would say that most public issues have religious implications. Aristotle defined politics as the art of making and keeping people truly human. Therefore, the Christian gospel must have something to say about our social, economic, and political affairs as well as our spiritual needs. By way of historic precedent John Wesley once said, "We have nothing to do but save souls," but he also said, "I have no religion but a social religion." And the revival of which he was a part made a unique contribution to the abolition of the slave trade, prison reform, and the birth and development of the labor party.

At the same time, the church and the individual Christian must practice humility. When some individual of limited experience offers a statement which would resolve war, eliminate poverty, and remove racism in one paragraph and then indicts everyone who doesn't embrace the same point of view, we wonder about that person's intelligence and integrity. The majority of people in politics are honorable, hardworking public servants who sincerely want to do a good job and probably have more experience than most who sit outside. We are often embarrassed by the self-righteous expressions and intolerant opinions of some church members.

There may come an occasional moment when the church as an institution must rise up and say to the state that it is not God; that its goals must be reexamined in the uncomfortable glare of biblical morality. There comes an occasional moment when the church as an institution must remind persons even in high places that they also stand under the judgment of God. We may not know how to offer political and military advice, but we can and must, on occasion, express moral outrage.

Albert Einstein, in an oft-quoted statement printed in the *New York Times*, said:

> As a lover of freedom, when the revolution came in Germany, I looked to the universities to defend it, knowing that they had always boasted of their devotion to the cause of truth; but no, the universities were immediately silenced. Then I looked to the great editors of the newspapers, whose flaming editorials in days gone by had proclaimed their love of freedom; but they, like the universities, were silenced in a few short weeks. Only the church stood squarely across the path of Hitler's campaign for suppressing truth. I never had any special interest in the church before, but now I feel a great affection and admiration for it, because the church alone has had the courage to stand for intellectual truth,

and moral freedom. I am forced to confess that what I once despised, now I praise unreservedly.

The church must speak because we believe that human knowledge is partial; only God is omniscient. We will come closer to the truth if there is open discussion, debate, and honest, responsible difference of opinion. No leaders are wise enough to foresee all the consequences of their action or to plan for every eventuality in the midst of complex and conflicting forces. We must have in a free society the equivalent of the British "loyal opposition."

Another reason for speaking out rests on the Christian assumption that all persons are possessed of sinful tendencies and are inclined to seek power or prestige for its own sake. This power must be checked and safeguards established so that the will of no person or group is beyond having someone question it.

We also have the conviction, established by the Nuremberg Trials after World War II, that there is a law higher than that of any nation. Our judges refused to accept the German defense that they were only obeying the law of their land and were innocent of any wrongdoing. Our officials appealed to a law higher than that of any nation and eliminated the normal appeals to the nature of war as justification for any act.

A Prophetic Voice

Let us consider the *second* question. What does it mean to be "prophetic" in our kind of world. In the effort to put faith and good works together there may be a few admonitions to keep in mind. In the first place, we must not pretend to have all the answers to the political and social ills that afflict our society. Jesus did not attempt to offer precise solutions for every issue. He demonstrated deep compassion for those in need but when asked about some political question he answered, "Render to Caesar the things that are Caesar's" (Mark 12:17). Ordination does not qualify a person to make judgments concerning political, economic, or international affairs. Ordained persons may qualify themselves in these fields by study and experience, but then the prophetic character is determined not by their status as clergy but by their qualifications in these areas of concern. And always, we must remember that decisions in economics and politics have to be made ultimately by the persons who actually bear the consequences of their decisions. We live in a democratic, pluralistic society. Persons of equal Christian commitment and wisdom may disagree with respect to specific issues. We must, therefore, not say, "Thus saith the Lord." We can surely say, "This is the way I see it. This is my best judgment." But we must know there are other persons, equally honest, equally able, who are committed to quite an opposite view.

Furthermore, the person who struggles to be "prophetic" is usually tempted to cite the example of the Old Testament prophets. While they were concerned about the social ills of the day, they were first of all trying to call their people back to a faith which was neglected, misunderstood, and distorted. We often quote out of context Isaiah's famous vision of a world at peace: "They shall beat their swords into plowshares" (2:4). But we neglect to mention that this universal peace is grounded in a vision of universal faith. It is only when the mountain of the Lord has been established that the nations will learn war no more.

There are all sorts of good deeds being accomplished out of splendid humanitarian motives. But the prophet is one who senses that righteousness is a result of religious revival. In a way, the person is right who insists that the preacher's first job is to talk about a person's relationship with God and from this new circumstance will come the motive to work on the social ills.

On one occasion a paralytic was brought to Jesus. He wanted to be healed. But Jesus first began talking about forgiving the man his sins. When some of his critics questioned his right to forgive sins, he answered by saying, "That you may know that the Son of man has authority on earth to forgive sins . . . I say to you, rise, take up your pallet and go home" (Mark 2:10-11). But his first concern was for the man's spiritual condition.

We must remember this. Much social reform is secular and humanistic. We can feed people until they are fat, clothe them elegantly, house them luxuriously, but it they do not have faith, and a right relationship with the Creator of Life, then the prophet has failed.

The prophetic person will believe in the power of moral persuasion. If a person of faith doesn't believe in the ultimate victory of love, who will? Secular society responds to others forces. Recently the personnel director of a large corporation and two of his associates invited four clergymen to have lunch with them. They explained in some detail the Equal Employment Opportunity Policy of their company and described what they call their "Affirmative Action Program." They said they were now doing many things they were not doing five years earlier. When asked what were the forces that brought about this change in climate, the answer given was this: First, government action—because the government expected certain hiring policies to prevail, they cooperated. Second, a period of full employment made it possible for them to dip down into what they would usually consider marginal groups; and third, the ethnic groups getting organized! Then the speaker continued, "I know you will be disappointed, but I don't think the church had much to do with it."

In other words, preaching human compassion had not made much difference. But riots, the threat of burning down the town, brought some swift changes in the hiring practices of a company that has been noted for its progressive policies. Someone has pointed out, "Poor, hurt, hungry people have nothing to gain from silence. Nobody rewards them for orderly behavior, for quiet acquiescence, for suffering in obscurity. Endless patience brings them nothing." Often this is tragically true. Nevertheless, we recall that when Jesus rode into Jerusalem to bring into the open, through confrontation, the evil that was entrenched, he refused to permit Peter to take a sword. He was fearless; he spoke out against hypocrisy. But he never used force except to drive the moneychangers out of the temple, and that is not a model for violence.

He was a revolutionary, but not in the sense of using violence. This is why the Jews rejected him. They wanted a military leader. He said, "Quit grumbling about the Roman occupation and win them through kindness." His method was often not so much civil disobedience as a kind of doubled-up civil obedience. Said he, "If any soldier of the occupation compels you to carry his equipment one mile, fool him, and carry it two!" But the whole style of his ministry was a rejection of actual violence.

In one of his speeches, Martin Luther King, Jr. said: "The ultimate weakness of violence is that it is a descending spiral, begetting the very thing it seeks to destroy. Returning violence for violence multiplies violence, adding deeper darkness to a night already devoid of stars. Darkness cannot drive out darkness: Only light can do that. Hate cannot drive out hate: Only love can do that." The real prophet must not forget this! Yet there are times when the Christian must act. Norman Mailer wrote in an autobiographical sketch, "How poor to go to death with no more than the notes of good intention. It is the actions of men and not their sentiments which make history."

In the mid-Forties, Nazi troops aroused Dietrich Bonhoeffer, marched him through the cool, springlike morning to the sandy courtyard, stripped him naked, and hanged him. Bonhoeffer was a quiet theologian, a pacifist, who loved his homeland intensely. Yet he had involved himself in the assassination plot on Hitler and plotted the downfall of his country. In so doing, he felt he was obedient to God. He was a visiting professor at Union Theological Seminary in New York City when the war came, and he returned home against the advice of his friends. He felt he had to do what he could to overthrow the Nazis so Western civilization could be preserved. He defined Christ as the man for others—the one who suffered for all persons. He felt the church had to suffer and sacrifice.

Jesus "went about doing good." He had what has been defined as the "posture of availability" but his actions were always out of love for God and humanity. This is the model for the contemporary prophet. Others may do it just because of a humanitarian impulse; the genuine prophet will do it out of love for God and humanity, and obedience to Christ.

CHAPTER TWELVE
ETERNAL LIFE

 lizabeth Kübler-Ross is a doctor who did an extensive study of the needs and attitudes of those who have a terminal illness. In an address to pastors she indicated that as she conducted her interviews, she soon discovered that questions were being raised she did not feel qualified to answer. Patients wanted to know what follows death. She asked a group of theological students to assist her in seeing the patients. Strangely, they did not seem to be of much help. She called them together and asked: "How many of you, without any shadow of doubt, believe in life after death?" When put that way, no one seemed confident enough to raise a hand. "I then knew," she said, "why they were unable to help the patients with their questions about life after death. They were using the right phrases, but their own uncertainty was coming through in the interviews with the terminally ill patients."

This doubt, while prevalent, is not in keeping with our heritage which affirms the life everlasting. In the Doctrinal Statement we read: "We gladly declare that the forgiveness of sins and life eternal are ours through the power of God's invincible love. . . . It is this love that defines our chief aim in life: 'to glorify God and to enjoy him forever.'"

While this theme does not occupy as large a place in preaching and Christian education as once accorded to it, the fact remains that central to Christian faith is the notion of eternal life. Our hymnal is rich with symbolism that testifies to the place of this theme in our corporate life. This is found not only in hymns but in our liturgical expressions, such as the Korean Creed, printed in our hymnal, which affirms: "We believe in the final triumph of righteousness, and in the life everlasting." The empty tomb and the life everlasting are always a part of our proclamation when we are faithful to the New Testament. The gospel, the "good news," is that God has acted in our behalf at the point of our mortality. There is the awesome reminder in scripture that "it is appointed for men to die once" (Heb. 9:27). The reality of our finitude makes us reach out for answers as to life's meaning. The span of life is so short, and frequently so heavy with burden, that we yearn for understanding and meaning and become convinced that only from the perspective of eternity can we see clearly its meaning.

Death comes to all, and is sometimes a welcome visitor, but what happens after death is a question that has haunted the human mind at least as long as recorded history. One fairly common belief is extinction. Death is the end. This inscription was found on an ancient Roman tomb: "I was not, and then I was born. Now, I am not and I care not."

Others believe in transmigration. This is notably true of some of the Eastern religions. According to this doctrine the soul transmigrates up or down into another body living on this earth. After death we may become a reptile or royalty. Our behavior in this life destines our body in the next.

Others believe in absorption. At death we are lifted up to one great prevailing spirit. Individual identity is lost. It is as a drop of water that falls into the ocean. There is continued existence, but not on an individual basis.

The Christian faith, however, has always affirmed a self-conscious existence beyond this life. In the year A.D. 125, a Greek by the name of Aristodes wrote to one of his friends about the new religion, Christianity. He was trying to explain the reasons for its extraordinary success. Here is a sentence from one of his letters:

> If any righteous man among the Christians passes from the world, they rejoice and offer thanks to God and they escort his body with songs and thanksgiving as if he were setting out from one place to another nearby.

A man who had lived his entire life within the church reached his eightieth birthday. At a dinner given him on that occasion, he arose and said:

> In my long life I have had many exciting adventures. I have

crossed the ocean numerous times, and have been around the world. But I am awaiting the greatest adventure of all, the journey into that land from which no traveler has ever returned.

That is the sort of faith with which a Christian faces the end of life. Now what's the basis for this confidence, this mood of assurance? Let us acknowledge that we cannot accumulate physical evidence for survival of bodily death that becomes convincing proof.

Nor can we advance an undeniable chain of logical argument, nor can we gain the kind of evidence that comes from weighing, counting, and measuring tangible things. But then there are remarkably few things that can be proved that way. Nothing can be proved about beauty, goodness, truth, honor, honesty, or love by these methods. Let us admit frankly that we are entering the realm of faith. And what we say is an attempt to reinforce the faith of the believing community. You can't persuade an unbeliever by argument. It can only be done by example and by that person's own hunger for certainty.

Faith in Forever

We advance four reasons for faith in the reality of continued self-conscious existence. The *first* reason is that there seems to be something in us that aspires after a life free of the mortal body.

For whatever reasons, sizable numbers of the human species have not lost a propensity for awe, for the uncanny. In a study of American students, published by Princeton Press, while only 48 percent admitted to a belief in God in traditional Judaeo-Christian terms, 80 percent expressed a "need for religious faith." In a similar study in Germany, while only 68 percent said they believed in God, 86 percent admitted to praying on occasion.

Peter Berger, a noted sociologist, says, "The human condition, fraught as it is with suffering and with the finality of death, demands interpretations that not only satisfy theoretically but give inner sustenance in meeting the crisis of suffering and death."

The *second* idea is the teleological argument, which is in fact an affirmation of faith. It begins from the assumption that this is a reasonable universe; that it has a purpose in it.

Consider the language of science. The fossils of the rocks and the various vegetable and animal species tell a story of countless ages devoted to the process of evolution. This process seems to be going somewhere. It looks as though it had a purpose. The end result of it all is human personality. In other words, our universe has lavished endless time and patience on the production of what we call personality. Does it make sense, then, to suppose that the universe after all this effort would suddenly turn around and blot out its most delicate creation? If you watched a skilled artisan spending twenty years in fashioning a particularly fine watch, would you expect him or her to let it run five minutes and then crush it to bits?

Some people find consolation in the thought that, even if individual persons do not live on, personality itself continues, in that parents have children and they have other children and so the process goes on and on. But sooner or later, this world of ours is likely to become a cold, blackened cinder unable any longer to support life. Then, the last generation will come to an end, and the last person on earth will die. When that happens, our noble experiment on this planet will be over. And what will it have amounted to? Exactly nothing. But we believe our universe makes sense. All along the line it acts as though it were "up to something." And if it has gone to so much trouble to create personality, it is likely to take lasting care of what it has made.

A *third* reason is that in this life we can never become what reason says we ought to become, and what we are meant to become; and, therefore, there must be another life so that we may complete our development. If ever we are to become what we are meant to be, this life is not enough.

Within the whole range of the world's literature we find no more constant theme than this disparity between human possibilities and aspirations on the one hand, and the narrow scope afforded us in the brief span of the present life. God never creates in us capacities for which there is no use. We are equipped with our minds, with our intuitions, and with our love for something greater than this life.

This idea that we must be made for something more than we can accomplish on this earth is illustrated by the dragonfly. Someone tells of sitting in a boat one day, near the shore, reading a book. Suddenly she was aware that a big, black beetle (actually a nymph) had come out of the water and crawled up on the boat. She looked over the side of the boat and could see there on the muddy bottom of the lake a score of these ugly little creatures. Under the heat of the sun, the nymph that had crawled out proceeded to die. Then a strange thing happened—his glistening black shell cracked down the back. Out of it came a shapeless mass whose hideousness was transformed into beautiful, brilliantly colored life. Out of the mass gradually unfolded four iridescent wings from which the sunlight flashed a thousand colors. The metamorphosis complete, this gorgeous dragonfly was soon dipping and soaring over the water. But the body it left behind still clung to the boat. And while the dragonfly happily explored its wonderful new world, its relatives still plodded below in the mire. Were they aware of the glorious creature flitting over their heads? Apparently not. But out of the mud had come a beautiful new life. If the Creator can work such wonders with the lowliest of creatures, should we not believe the human spirit will have another world in which to expand, free from the limitations of the body? Paul said: "This mortal nature must put on immortality" (1 Cor. 15:53).

The *fourth* reason for our belief is that as Christians we have faith in the character of God as set forth in the life and teaching of Jesus. We begin with the faith that God is a heavenly parent, and we are the children. If this is true, then God cares for us. And if God truly cares for us, this concern lasts not just a little while but always. We can say of God as had been said of Jesus: "Having loved his own . . . he loved them to the end" (John 13:1). Then nothing, not even death, can take us out of the heavenly house or beyond the reach of God's continuous care.

It would be a heartless parent who would make us in his/her own image, rear us into self-conscious sons and daughters, develop our personalities capable of thinking high thoughts and planning noble deeds, permit us to dream dreams of a life that has no end—and then after a very few years snuff us out as one blows out a candle. It is inconceivable that God, who is supremely good, just and loving should allow those who offer their lives in service, to perish as if they had never been.

Eternal Life Is Like . . .

What is this life on the other side of what we call death to be like? What kind of bodies will we have? How shall we put in our time?

Frankly, it is not easy to extract from the New Testament any kind of clear and coherent statement of what happens after death.

The traditional view within Protestantism has always been that those who believe will share eternally the bliss of fellowship with God in heaven, while those who refuse God's love are eternally separated into the misery of hell. This position takes human responsibility quite seriously but the notion of eternal separation from God for some persons is hard to reconcile with the Christ-like character of God.

The Confession of Faith of the former Evangelical United Brethren Church, adopted in 1962, asserts in Article XII, "We believe all men stand under the righteous judgment of Jesus Christ, both now and in the last day. We believe in the resurrection of the dead; the righteous to life eternal and the wicked to endless condemnation." In the more recent doctrinal statement, something of the preciseness of this earlier confession is lost. There is little hint of future reward and punishment but a simple statement that we believe in the life eternal through the power of God's invincible love.

The matter of heaven and hell has loomed large in Christian teaching through the centuries and cannot be ignored. Yet the New Testament gives little information, and what we do find there is symbolic suggestion. One symbol for hell is that used by Jesus when he made reference to the valley south of Jerusalem where the city's waste was dumped. This would remind us that hell is for those who have made themselves useless to God. Paul reminds us in Romans 6:23: "The wages of sin is death, but the free gift of God is eternal life in Christ Jesus our Lord."

The New Testament generally suggests that life after death is a continuation of life before death but on what is called a spiritual level. In this sense, eternal life is something that is given here and continues after death. If we grow in grace, in love and knowledge of God here, it shall continue afterward. If we are in rebellion here, then we shall continue to experience separation there. The goal of Christians is to do our best in fellowship here and leave to God what will be done for us beyond this earthly life. But we do insist that how we live here makes a difference in the world to come. Perhaps heaven and hell are appropriate symbols, or perhaps they no longer convey meaningful imagery because of the distortions associated with these terms in the Middle Ages. Nevertheless, we do believe that the quality of our life now has an eternal dimension. Jesus said, "Not every one who says to me, 'Lord, Lord,' shall enter the kingdom of heaven" (Matthew 7:21). We must therefore respond in faith and love, live responsibly and in obedience, and thus come with confident trust to the close of life knowing we can hear those beauteous words, "Come, O blessed of my Father, inherit the kingdom prepared for you from the foundation of the world" (Matthew 25:34).

Another view is described as conditional immortality. Immortality is not a quality of the human soul but a gift of God. The scripture confirms this. "This gift of God is life eternal." Those who persist in opposing God's purpose of love cut themselves off from the source of eternal life and simply cease to be.

Another view widely held is that of universalism. This says that all persons will finally be restored to God. It rests mainly upon those New Testament passages which affirm the triumph of the God who does not desire that any should perish. It believes that God will find a way of reconciling all persons without destroying their freedom.

Without attempting to describe the next life too precisely, here is what many United Methodists have come to believe scripture and human intuition confirm.

First, eternal life begins now. Within this world of space and time we can enter into a relationship with God, and it lasts forever simply because God is God. Human relationships can be and are broken. People drift apart. Death comes between. But to be in relationship with God is to be in a relationship which cannot be broken in death. When death comes, we simply move on to another plane, but the relationship continues unbroken and uninterrupted.

Toward the end of his life when Jesus was trying to prepare his disciples for his separation from them, he said, "Let not your hearts be troubled; believe in God, believe also in me. In my Father's house are many rooms" (John 14:1-2). That is really all we need to know. This present life is one room in the Father's house. The life beyond is another room in the same house. We don't need to know precisely where that room is, or what it looks like, or the kind of furniture it will contain. All we need to know is that it is a part of the Father's house, and his love and care are in control there as they are here.

Second, nothing short of eternal life is consistent with the character and purpose of God. But how is this possible? We know life only through a physical body and the body is mortal. Without a body, how can there be life after death? Actually, we do not hold to the Greek notion that the soul is a separate entity from the body and at death is set free to enter the presence of God. We believe the New Testament affirms that life after death is by resurrection; God giving us a body like Christ's glorious body. In fact, the first chapter of Romans reminds us that the resurrection-power is already at work within us and this is the meaning of "eternal life." It is something that starts now. And the interrelation of body and soul in this life supports the concept that in the life to come we shall have "spiritual bodies" and not be disembodied spirits. All of this, of course, is a mystery. If the child in the womb were capable of self-consciousness, it could not imagine what life would be like in the world into which it enters at birth. It is beyond the range of its experience. In similar fashion, our limited experience does not qualify us to understand all the intuitions, feelings, aspirations, hopes, and dreams that possess us. It is beyond what we can know or explain even though we are utterly convinced that there is "more beyond." But we do believe we will have a "spiritual body."

Third, this life eternal will be characterized by continued growth and development. For many centuries the Catholic branch of Christendom has taught the doctrine of purgatory. Protestantism has always rejected this, and many Roman Catholic scholars have drawn back from some of the excessive interpretations. It was the abuse of this doctrine which moved Luther in part to initiate the actions which resulted in the Reformation.

United Methodists have rightly rejected the idea that salvation is something we win by our own merits. Eternal life is God's gift, resulting from a relationship established with the heavenly creator in this life. Yet, I can't but feel that there must be some measure of truth in the idea that we will continue to grow, develop, abandon faulty attitudes of spirit, and go through a process of purification before we have the capacity to enjoy full fellowship with the Lord of all created things.

Obviously, we are in the presence of a mystery. There is much we cannot know in this life. Let us rest content in the knowledge that the Gospels come to a climax in the resurrection as a dramatic way of saying that it is God's will that we enter into life eternal. Jesus said, "Because I live, you will live also" (John 14:19). This is all the promise we need for the present. Our duty is to receive in faith the gracious gift of God's redeeming love and yield our lives in joyous obedience to the Lord's will while trusting the future to God's care.

When Singapore fell to the Japanese in 1942, Mrs. Rogers Mulvaney, a Canadian, was working there for the Red Cross. Along with more than four thousand other civilians she was locked in Changi jail which had been built to accommodate four hundred and fifty prisoners. They suffered four years of crowding and hunger, loneliness and isolation, with no news of families and home.

As the first Easter approached, Mrs. Mulvaney went to the guards and asked if they might sing hymns in the courtyard on Easter morning. At first they were refused, but were finally given permission to sing for five minutes. In the presence of one guard they sang for five precious minutes, praising God for Christ's resurrection, the only hope to which they could cling. Then silently they marched back. But as Mrs. Mulvaney entered the passageway, the guard stepped up, reached under his brown shirt, drew out a tiny orchid and placing it in her hand softly spoke, "Christ *did* rise." Then with a smart military about-face, he was gone. But Mrs. Mulvaney stood there, eyes brimming with tears, knowing that she and the others need never again feel forsaken. To know this is to know eternal life now.

CHAPTER THIRTEEN

LAST THINGS

"nited Methodists, along with all other Christians, are a pilgrim people under the Lordship of Christ." This phrase from the Doctrinal Statement sets the stage for this paragraph: "We are called to proclaim and live out the eternal gospel in an age of catastrophic perils and soaring hopes. Humanity stands nearer the brink of irreversible disaster than ever before. Our reckless disregard of nature's fragile balances, our rush to over-population, pollution, the exhaustion of basic ecological support systems, the proliferation of nuclear weaponry go on unchecked.... At the same time, visions of a more fully human quality of life for all mankind haunt our imaginations and stir our aspirations as never before.... We who are caught up in this perplexing situation seek to understand our Christian faith and interpret it to others."

Do we know where we are going? Does history have a destination, or will it just come to the end of the line? Someone has defined history as "the succession of one thing after another." Taken seriously, this assumes that history is not going anywhere and has no ultimate goal or purpose.

It is reported that John Wanamaker once said: "I know half the money I spend on advertising is wasted, but I can never find out which half." So we could acknowledge that much of our activity is unprofitable, but which part? Somewhere, we continue to hope, there must be a clue which will give meaning to it all. We are on the road, we are engulfed in activity, but where are we going? Is it to the end of the line, or to a destination? We continue to play our parts, but we want to comprehend the play.

Popular Views

Most of the popular conceptions about the goal of history would suggest that things just go on until we come to the end of the line.

One such theory develops the idea that we will continue our "little round" until history reaches its end with an uninhabitable earth. Astronomers tell us that the sun will end human life. There is every reason to believe that, at some future point in time, physical conditions will no longer be conducive to the continuance of human life. While we may accept this as an inevitable reality, it tells us little about the meaning of life in its present form.

If history is nothing but going in the same old pattern until this earth ceases to be habitable, then many of the things we do are without lasting significance and might well be omitted. But we hasten to add that the Christian need not capitulate to this theory about history with its inevitable cynicism which dissipates purposeful endeavor. Honest deliberation and prayerful searching will soon reveal the poverty of this answer.

Another possibility is that our ingenuity will end human life before the sun can do it. We wait with a kind of vague anxiety for the thing to blow up. We now speak of "overkill." Russia boasts that it has the nuclear capability of destroying our nation one hundred and fifty times. By some ironic twist of reasoning, we seem to feel more secure because we can retort that we have the capacity for destroying Russia five hundred times! What difference does it make after the first time?

A recent President of the United States said the sword of Damocles hangs over the world. Damocles, who lived in the fourth century before Christ, once insulted King Dionysius of Syracuse. He was condemned by the king to attend a royal banquet and sit beneath a naked sword that was suspended by a single hair. We are under such a sword. It is swinging back and forth and the hair is getting more and more frayed with every passing day. In 1962, when we put our mines in the harbor at Haiphong, we waited, tense and anxious, to see what the Russian ships would do. We knew that, if they confronted our mines with a showdown, we might have come to the end of the line.

The Bishop's Pastoral Letter "In Defense of Creation," offered to the church in 1986, was an effort to reduce the nuclear threat and avoid a politics of confrontation.

History's weariness with human factionalism can easily lead to despair. The adherents of nihilism are apparently justified in their stance. In the preface of one of Winston Churchill's books, he writes: "I have called this volume triumph and tragedy, because the overwhelming victory of the Grand Alliance has failed so far to bring peace to our anxious world." Our self-destructive tendencies, most dramatically portrayed in our repetitive and meaningless wars, give credence to the conclusion that our ingenuity will end human life. Christians, however, cannot embrace this as *their* answer to the enigma of history.

If history does not end with the nuclear bang, there are those who think it will come to the end of the line in an existential whimper! There is ample confusion and tension in our present situation. There is an evergrowing assault upon our traditional social conventions. Morality seems to be established through a statistical equation. In blunt terms, this means that the adults are saying, as do the youngsters: "It's all right if everyone is doing it." There is a revolt against discipline which manifests itself in literature, art, drama, and music. There is a massive disillusionment with the old systems. The beliefs and practices of Protestantism, capitalism, and our political system generally are all under attack. The forces of social change are often beyond the bounds of moral and rational behavior. Rifle brigades, vigilantes, coercion, retaliation, boycott, intimidation—this is the language of social ferment.

Are these tensions and expressions the birth pangs of a new and better society? Are they the death struggles of a history that is coming to the end of the line? Frankly, we don't know. History does inform us, however, that civilizations which tried to flee from their confusions and conflicts by absorbing themselves in the product of a sensate culture soon perished! This is dying with a whimper.

A newspaper recently carried a provocative article about Western civilization, with particular reference to our own nation. It began: "The test of a great civilization is not its mechanical gadgets . . . it is rather a matter of imponderables, such as delight in the things of the mind, of beauty, honor, grace, courtesy, and delicate feeling." It went on to illustrate how far we have drifted. Out of its many references I shall select only one: "In one state, Nevada, we gamble away more money in a single year than we spend nationally on medical research.

As a nation we spend thirty-three billion dollars on gambling, more than we spend on the entire educational system—kindergarten to university. We are a nation whose bookies outnumber its physicians." Does this sound like a society that should be preserved? This frantic pursuit of the gambling craze grows out of our subconscious conviction that, since nothing significant is ultimately possible in history, we should take minor gratifications from the perishing moments. Persuaded that the struggle is without meaning, we avidly seek momentary escape and diversion.

The Meaning of Life

I know there is an apparent irrationality about life. Lew Ayers' death in *All Quiet on the Western Front* illustrates this. After surviving until the end of the war, he is killed by the enemy when he reaches out of a trench for a butterfly. Our impoverished understandings, however, must not lead us to search from meaning in the offerings of a society of overabundance. There is agony, but there can also be ecstasy. There is high adventure if we move toward the rich affirmation of human destiny. There is much more in the Christian answer than the negative conclusions that history will collapse from the fat of its own self-indulgence.

I think the reason for our inability to arrive at an answer is simple. An answer cannot arise from human logic because our perspective is too limited. No one has experienced the end of history. It is, therefore, impossible to reach ultimate conclusions through the facility of the human mind. We turn, then, to an examination of the Christian affirmation which grows, not out of logic, but out of a profound declaration of faith, based upon revelation. Here is our premise.

The Christian faith assumes that the historical process is known in its entirety by God, who created both the process and the people who take part in it. Furthermore, we believe that God entered human history, and in the life, teaching, death, and resurrection of Jesus Christ revealed the significance of the historical enterprise.

This does not make much sense if we seek answers that are logical from our human perspective. The Christian declaration has always involved the dimension of faith as a response to the revelation of God. The gospel is a proclamation that comes to the world and some "get it" while others do not. To those who do, it is "the power of God unto salvation." To those who do not, it is a scandal and an offense.

The Christian view of history, furthermore, insists upon a linear concept rather than the hopeless cyclical repetition of "one thing after another." This understanding of history can be visualized as a line which begins with creation, centers on the redemptive act of God in Jesus Christ, and finds its termination in sanctifying final judgment.

When we speak of creation, we are not primarily concerned with when and how this happened. These are questions for science to answer. Our statement grows out of a realization that God did it, and did it that all people might have a purposeful relationship with the eternal creator.

From creation, we move to redemption. Humanity's rebellion broke the harmonious relationship which had existed between creator and created. "God was in Christ reconciling." The great act of self-giving love becomes the center of history. Love makes loss devastatingly real, because it lies at the very heart of life and death. The love of God, revealed in the act of the cross, displays the meaning of history and becomes the criterion for interpreting all other acts.

The Christian stance affirms that history has a destination in that it is moving toward a judgment that is final and perfect. We do not often preach and teach about an ultimate judgment. We are not certain as to what we should conclude from those scriptural passages which speak of judgment. We cannot avoid, however, the necessity of a final and perfect judgment at the end of time which will give history a direction, an ultimate meaning, and a destination. For the Christian the end of time does not hold terror, but anticipation. It is a time when inequity is set right. It is a moment of revelation when we shall understand the purpose of the struggle. It is the act wherein those who are in Christ will move from an incomplete relationship to one that is perfect and whole. By faith, we shall see the One who died to redeem us from the hell of our own self-seeking and who restored us to meaningful life which by definition is life lived in obedience to the law and will of God. In the meantime, the life which we live in Christ in the here and now will have the elements of change, choice, and confidence.

Resources for Further Reading

The following titles are available from Discipleship Resources, P.O. Box 189, 1908 Grand Avenue, Nashville, Tennessee 37202 (615-340-7285).

THE UNITED METHODIST PRIMER
This new and enlarged edition of a Discipleship Resources classic tells the story of our faith as United Methodist Christians, our particular heritage, our beliefs, our membership in the church, our ministry as individuals and as congregations, and our church organization. The *Primer* is especially useful for those inquiring about United Methodist membership and for new members. Chester E. Custer has written an ideal text for a membership training class and current members will benefit by this overview of the faith and the church. This helpful resource interprets the basic theological beliefs and membership vows, with special attention to their implications for an active ministry of the laity in United Methodist churches, communities, and the world. (No. DR024B)

THE UNITED METHODIST WAY
A booklet giving a brief overview of United Methodist history, beliefs, organization, and mission (including an interpretation of the membership vows). Especially suitable as a gift for new or prospective members or in membership training classes. By Branson Thurston. (No. M254K)

CONOZCA LA IGLESIA METODISTA UNIDA
The United Methodist Way
Este interesante librito presenta en forma clara y amena un resumen de la historia, creencias, misión y organización de la Iglesia Metodista Unida. Es ideal para miembros nuevos o para quien desee conocer en poco tiempo estos aspectos de nuestra Iglesia. (No. F083K)

ESSENTIAL BELIEFS FOR UNITED METHODISTS

James Hares develops the Wesleyan emphasis "revealed in *scripture,* illumined by *tradition,* verified in *personal experience,* and confirmed by *reason* as an experimental approach to our essential beliefs." (No. M206K)

COMO FORMULA SUS CREENCIAS LA IGLESIA METODISTA UNIDA

Essential Beliefs for United Methodists

Después de una introducción histórica, el autor explica en forma clara y amena las cuatro guías en que se basan los metodistas unidos para sus creencias: la Biblia, la tradición, la experiencia y la razón. Este librito está especialmente adaptado para el pueblo hispano. Por James Hares. (No. F082K)

OUR JOURNEY: A WESLEYAN VIEW OF THE CHRISTIAN WAY

Based on the experience and theology of John Wesley, Maxie Dunnam presents a guide to the path of faith: our hope for salvation, our sin, God's amazing grace forgiving and renewing us, the gift of assurance, the continuing path toward perfect love, the church as Christ's dwelling place, personal and social holiness, the disciplines of the Christian, and the distinctive style of the people called Methodist. Many modern illustrations aid individual or group study. (No. DR013B)

QUESTIONS ASKED BY UNITED METHODISTS

Bishop Mack B. Stokes' response, in narrative form, to questions being asked by many United Methodists concerning the Bible, God, Man, Jesus Christ, the Holy Spirit, Justification, Assurance, the New Birth, Sanctification, Responsible Living, the Church, Eternal Life, and the Origins and Specific Doctrines of The United Methodist Church. (No. M238B)

RESPUESTAS A PREGUNTAS QUE HACEN LOS METODISTAS UNIDOS

Questions Asked by United Methodists

El Obispo Mack B. Stokes usa el método de preguntas y respuestas para explicar en forma breve y concisa una variedad de temas, como Dios, el Ser Humano, Jesucristo, el Espíritu Santo, la Biblia, la Iglesia, la Vida Eterna, etc. (No. F026B)